EMBRACING
THE UNKNOWN

EMBRACING THE UNKNOWN

Exploring the Pathways to Change

LISA DeANGELIS

NEW DEGREE PRESS
COPYRIGHT © 2022 LISA DeANGELIS
All rights reserved.

EMBRACING THE UNKNOWN
Exploring the Pathways to Change

The poem "Pathways" is printed with permission from its author, Leah Fortner.

ISBN
979-8-88926-658-7   *Paperback*
979-8-88926-659-4   *Digital Ebook*

For all those brave enough to embrace the journey toward their unknown, and to every amazing human who has supported me in mine.

Contents

INTRODUCTION	Starting Here	9
PART I	**WHY CHANGE?**	**17**
CHAPTER 1	Change or Be Changed	19
CHAPTER 2	The Illusion of Control	31
CHAPTER 3	Tools for Change	47
CHAPTER 4	Into the Unknown	59
PART II	**CHANGING NOW**	**73**
CHAPTER 5	Caution: Change in Progress	75
CHAPTER 6	Step Into Stretch	85
CHAPTER 7	Permission to Launch	99
CHAPTER 8	A View from Above	111
CHAPTER 9	The Change Cycle	123
PART III	**CHANGING FOREVER**	**135**
CHAPTER 10	It's Not a Diet; It's a Lifestyle	137
CHAPTER 11	A—Authenticity: Our Truth	145
CHAPTER 12	L—Learning: Back to the Basics	157
CHAPTER 13	I—Intentionality: The Art of the Pivot	173
CHAPTER 14	G—Gratitude: The Constant Gardener	185
CHAPTER 15	N—Nurture: Becoming	199
CONCLUSION	Getting "There"	213

Acknowledgments	217
About the Author	223
Appendix	225

INTRODUCTION

Starting Here

My mind reeled. It felt like a scene in a movie where the sound blurs, and everything goes silent. The camera rolls in for a close-up of my face. A scared girl sits tensely in a cold, beige leather chair. She feels utterly alone, and a million thoughts run through her head.

Reconstructive jaw surgery?

The specialist made clear there wasn't any other way to determine what was happening. "We'll have to go in, take everything apart, figure out what's going on and try to address it, then put it all back together again." He paused. "Assuming everything goes well, you should regain full functioning when all is said and done. Of course, there's never an absolute guarantee."

Assuming? Should? No guarantee? I was a singer! Only eighteen at the time, I had just finished my first semester in college, studying voice. My whole life was ahead of me. *And if it doesn't go well?* My racing mind read between the blurry lines: I might not be able to eat or talk, let alone sing again. It felt like a bad dream.

A deafening silence filled the room, numbing my body. My mom sat on my left, listening intently as the doctor spoke. Words continued coming out of his mouth, but I didn't hear any of them. If I had one wish at that moment, it was to be plucked out of that chair and dropped somewhere—anywhere—else.

What I feared most was change. Yet, with sharp clarity, I sensed a deep knowing. Only I could make this decision. The doctor's idea about surgery was too far out of my comfort zone—for good reason. But I wasn't sure what "change" would mean for my life.

It's been over twenty years since that day, and I now recognize change isn't something to be feared. In fact, I've learned an incredible amount about embracing and creating effective change in my life.

In today's world, the health and survival of any system, organization, or person depends on their ability to change and adapt. But we (humans especially) can be surprisingly resistant to change. A crippling fear of the unknown leads people to stay in jobs and relationships where they aren't happy for far too long. We might not take that risk, try something new, or talk to a stranger in the line at the grocery store, missing opportunities for growth, shift, or connection. We stick to safe, comfortable routines, day after day, week after week, year after year—sometimes without even realizing it.

As quickly as we blink, things can change. We exist in a world where inflation is at an all-time high, and the call for social change is too loud to ignore. Technology has become an integral part of our lives and is being adopted at a dizzying pace.

Although it took approximately forty-five years for landline phones to show up in 50 percent of US households, it only took four years for smartphones to reach 40 percent of them (DeGusta 2020).

The world keeps moving. Chronic overstimulation has made it easy to become numb, leaving us unsure of how to approach change. Over time, well-worn daily routines may have created deep ruts along our path. Maybe we're not making progress in our careers or aren't happy with our personal lives. Running on autopilot, one day we wake up to realize we've started to rust because we're not changing.

Everyone thinks change is what happens to us or something we do. I think change is a choice. It's about rediscovering the optimal tools and conditions for changing, adopting them as a mindset, and living them as intentional choices.

Change is a fluid process of stretching ourselves. Establishing resources that support change helps leverage permission and perspective to optimize freedom of choice and opportunity. We hone and strengthen these skills of change by learning to identify the when, where, and what to stretch. This allows us to achieve the results we want, both now and in our lives as they unfold.

Sitting in that doctor's chair at eighteen, my life unfolded in some unexpected ways. Who would have thought a cold and sterile room, a chair that felt like it might swallow me, and a doctor wearing a long white coat would set the scene for such a significant shift? Gurus and sages throughout history have referenced the "still, small voice" inside us all. At that moment, my inner voice was neither still nor small. I received one of the clearest messages I've ever gotten.

I didn't get the surgery.

Because of that choice, I still searched for a solution to my jaw problem. That's how I found the Alexander Technique, a holistic body reeducation method, and my teacher Stacy. Over the years, Stacy became both a mentor and friend, teaching me more about life through our weekly lessons than I could have imagined. On the surface, our work together addressed my posture, alignment, and body use (jaw issues included), but it was so much more.

She helped me learn how to harness the power of my thinking. I realized I didn't even know why I made some of the choices I did:

- Did I really need to stand on my toes, arching my back, when I sang? (It made my jaw problem worse.)
- Why was it so hard to sit down without plopping into a chair? (I didn't even know I did this!)
- What else was I doing because of habit and not by choice? (This one took a bit more time.)

I learned to let go of what I didn't need to hold on to. That paved the way for me to show up in the world differently. I had been introduced to principles for meaningful change and lasting freedom of choice. Eventually, I trained as a teacher of the Alexander Technique myself and have worked with these principles of change, applying them throughout my professional career and personal life.

Although I didn't realize it at eighteen, I was in an optimal space for change. As a college freshman, I had my first taste of autonomy in the world, stretching myself in ways I hadn't before. There was space (and permission) to make my own decisions. I was also given the gift of an entirely new perspective. The tools and resources of this space allowed me to explore my life through a new lens. I understood, even when I wasn't sure how, I *did* have a choice.

Change is, and always will be, hard. There's no sugarcoating this. I know because I've experienced change and continue to live it. At scary career transition points, it's difficult to decide which choice to make. I've walked away from opportunities that seemed perfect from the outside. I've felt gnawing nudges and followed deep inner pulls, knowing there's been more. At times, I've struggled desperately to see in the dark. Life's big decisions can take us in new directions, and that is a daunting proposition.

I haven't written this book to present myself as an authority or expert in change but as a regular person who understands from experience that change is a flow of action we can choose at any moment. I started out to solve a very different problem. I committed to discovering what I didn't know, unsure of what I might learn. Seeds of curiosity were planted, and experience moved into action. I took the first step toward embracing the unknown on an indirect pathway to change. This choice activated and catalyzed growth. I never imagined this would have led me on such a journey.

I've read countless books and worked out these ideas over years of conversations, research, and experience. Bringing together my interests in various disciplines—including neuroscience, the Alexander Technique, and the wisdom of the natural world—resulted in me seeing the experience of change through new eyes. Returning after gathering knowledge, information, and understanding, I recognize my pathways are constantly shifting and expanding. These learnings can help others discover where they want to go or can be a support in the exploration of the pathways that lead to lasting and sustainable change.

The important tools of change are more accessible than people think. I'll share what octopuses and ants can teach us, how we can use research on habit and fear to help form new pathways forward, and how shifts in thinking can pave the way for new opportunities. As counterintuitive as it may seem, sometimes doing less—including stopping and creating space—helps eliminate barriers and allows for more intentional decision-making.

I'll provide a framework for exploring and embracing the tools for change and living in a cycle that supports our ongoing growth and emergence. In choosing our path forward, we reclaim the ability to live a life truly *aligned* with change. Embracing the unknown can lead to things that aren't bullet-pointed on our lists, and the possibility of change emerges for those who engage with these ideas.

You are the only one who can change your life. And although it might not be easy, it will be worth it.

Pathways

There are infinite paths to choose,
And I have chosen many.
I have slammed into dead ends,
Twisted through turning trails that ended at lost,
Followed other's routes to eventually realize they weren't mine,
Even dared to venture into the great unknown,
Where writing a new way,
Was the only way.
But of all the countless roads I wandered,
Endless directions I explored,
And limitless possibilities I could have taken,
There is one thing I have come to know:
No matter what surrounds me,
Lies ahead or behind me,
Or who is beside me,
It's what is happening in me,
That will shine a guiding light,
Conquer the journey,
And land me victorious after any travel.
Because perfection comes,
not when you're watching golden sunsets over paradise,
But when you have grown,
Unbreakable,
At peace,
Within.

—Leah Fortner

PART I

WHY CHANGE?

"Human beings are works in progress that mistakenly think they're finished."

—DAN GILBERT

CHAPTER 1

Change or Be Changed

The view was stunning. Puffy white clouds peppered the clear blue sky, and the sun cast a warm glow across the mountaintops. I looked out over the horizon. Snowcaps in the distance sparkled as the light danced on their peaks. My breathing was still slightly labored from the climb, but each step it took to reach the top had been more than worth the effort.

"Wow." The word escaped my lips more like a reverent exhale than an exclamation.

A soft breeze brushed across my cheek, and the lids of my eyes gently closed as I soaked in the warmth of the sun. I took a deep breath, sensing the clean air that filled my lungs. I wanted to stop time—capture this moment.

I quickly leaned down to search for my backpack. It sat crumpled on the ground next to me, where I had haphazardly shaken it off my back when I reached the summit. I fumbled through and triumphantly found my camera. But when I stood up to take the picture, I realized the sun had already disappeared behind the endless sheets of rapidly moving clouds.

Shoot. I missed it.

A moment later, as if someone had continued turning the wheel of the most colorful kaleidoscope I'd ever seen, the view changed again. I watched as the sun continued to play hide-and-seek. I realized I could see even more depth of color in the landscapes all around me in the sun's absence. Feeling insignificant amid such grandeur, I wasn't sure I needed the picture. At that moment, I was part of the vast landscape. No photo could capture the sensation. I stood there and took another deep breath, soaking in as much of the moment as possible.

The only constant in life is change. An aphorism ascribed to the Greek philosopher Heraclitus, this fact has brought me hope in times of sorrow and grief in moments of deep joy. When I want nothing more than to change, it offers relief. Yet, in times when things have been good, it's been a somewhat frustrating—even annoying—fact. More than once, I've wanted to stop time. *Can't I just hold on to this moment? Why does everything have to change?*

What I find most interesting about Heraclitus isn't just this inevitability of change he so simply states; it's how he goes on to express the entire *experience* of change: No man ever steps into the same river twice (Robinson 1978, 55). Ever-flowing water means it's never the same river; from moment to moment, we are never the same person. We are constantly changing, shifting, and moving. There's a natural ebb and flow to all the cycles of life, right down to some of the most essential actions.

Take breath, for example. On any given day, your body will breathe itself an average of twenty thousand times—and no two breaths are the same. "Kind of like snowflakes!" one of my teachers once said. Most of us hardly think much about something that happens as subconsciously as breathing. But what if we could? What if we did? How many times throughout a single day could we enjoy a breath? Could we get a little more tuned in to whatever happens next? Through choice, this simple act of connection turns into a moment we can relish.

There's both power and humility when we step back and realize "change" isn't so much a verb that describes a moment in time as a constant—a state of being. Yet, we are surprisingly resistant to change. Or perhaps a clarification: we are resistant to *being changed*.

Anna was a creature of habit. She had a tight routine that ran her mornings: coffee, workout, shower, a little news while she ate breakfast, and it was out the door. Her car ride allowed her to clear her head most mornings on the commute. The perky voice of the radio show host offered comic relief, and she knew exactly what to expect once she got to the building. She'd wave hello to the front desk security and nod politely as she waited for the elevator.

She squeezed into the boardroom just a moment before the company-wide meeting began that Monday morning, sliding easily into one of the last open seats in the room. She recalls, "I expected it to be like all the other meetings. I didn't expect—certainly didn't want—anything to be *changing*."

Her boss went on to explain there would be broad restructuring changes over the coming weeks. Managers would be meeting with all employees individually to discuss details. In the meantime, everyone's patience and flexibility were requested. She had heard some rumors and mumblings around the office that a merger was possible, but no one thought it would be happening so soon. She hadn't considered team changes might be involved.

Although it took time, her team built a good rapport. She was a natural leader and tried to maintain a sense of optimism despite their obstacles. Nervously reflecting on her performance in the previous quarter, she reminded herself that everyone had been struggling lately. In this unknown, she wasn't sure what all this talk of change ultimately meant.

Organizational change management has been studied and researched extensively in the business world. If companies don't change, adapt, and stay relevant, they risk the threat of not only failure or bankruptcy but also obscurity. New businesses are forming at record rates. From 2010 to 2020, there was a 75 percent increase in the yearly number of new business applications, and 2021 held a current record, with over 5.4 million applications filed in the calendar year (US Census Bureau 2019). As new companies and concepts arise, their choices reflect the fluid nature of the business world.

Where once sprawling malls and large stores dominated the marketplace, newer companies have shown up with fresh ideas and business models that maximize both their brand and customer reach. The direct-to-consumer shoe brand Margaux began with pop-up locations in their desired markets. A few years after their 2015 launch, they opened a flagship store in New York City's West Village. Although you can go in to browse their collection and determine your size, you won't be walking out with a new pair that day. After your "Cinderella moment" to find the perfect fit, your shoes are purchased in the store and shipped directly to your home. This ability to reduce on-site stock maximizes resources while maintaining a high level of individualized service to each customer.

Or take a brand like Duluth Trading Company. Initially a catalog company catered to the construction industry, over time, creative marketing and product expansion led to increased product offerings, including a clothing line for women. When many retail stores were closing or downsizing in the mid-2010s, Duluth embraced the opposite approach and opened its first brick-and-mortar retail stores. As other concepts were downsizing, they scaled up. Whenever changes to their concept were made, they continually trusted their brand's vision and met with tremendous success.

Organizational change for businesses is not just about following trends but developing brands, products, advertising, and strategies that meet the constantly shifting needs of the world around them. Kurt Lewin, widely considered a leader in organizational change management, explored and detailed a three-step change model that's been adapted and applied in many scenarios and is still often used today. Lewin's model presents changing in three simple steps: Unfreezing, Moving, and Refreezing (Lewin 1947).

As we unfreeze and thaw, we become open and available to move—to change. Change happens, and then we refreeze, working to solidify the shift. Sort of like an ice cube, the state of frozen water changes forms in various scenarios or under certain conditions. Thaw, change, and refreeze happens in cycles. Supported by the correct big-picture thinking, this process takes us closer to where we want to be. The motivations for change, as well as the results that come from fitting together the various pieces of the puzzle, all contribute to this field of organizational change management. Although overly simplistic, these (and other) frameworks are routinely applied and utilized in complex business systems. Their effects can be seen in organizations and their cultures, as well as applied to leaders, best practices, and even employees.

What about when it comes to us as individuals and our personal journeys of change? We, too, are a complex system. But instead of many players on the field working together as a team, we are the team; the whole complex system rolled up into one. We are an organization with a five-year or even ten-year plan, working to stay relevant in an ever-changing world. We are the leaders, responsible for the visionary choices and big-picture thinking, paving the way toward where we want to go. And we're the employees too. We are doing the grunt work and getting down into the little details, often having to ensure all the t's are crossed and the i's are dotted. As individuals, we also need whole system thinking—and tools—when considering the long-game approach, especially when the world around us changes at a record pace.

Take the world of social media over the last eighteen years. In 2005, just 6 percent of adults aged thirty to forty-nine used a social media site. By 2021, that statistic grew to a whopping 81 percent (Pew Research Center 2021). Many people who previously claimed they'd never use social media now utilize multiple platforms daily just to stay connected. We're shocked at the price of groceries or gas but don't have much of a choice. We simply do our best to stay on top of the latest trends and keep ourselves prepared. Without the ability to see the future, we don't know with certainty what's ahead. And that doesn't always feel great.

Growing up, my cousins and I were relegated to stories that began with "When I was your age…" or "Back when I was a kid…." Clinging to how it "used to be" offered a stark contrast to how things now were. Does it do us any good to live in the past? Things that have been around longer seem to offer us a sense of dependability—even if that's not the reality. We still believe the longer something is thought to exist, the better it inherently is. Without even realizing it, we have a bias toward more established things. Participants in a 2010 study on a bias of longevity were presented with the same art piece. One group was told it was created in 2005, the other in 1905. Participants in the 1905 group rated the painting much more aesthetically pleasing. Similar results came when looking at the validity of acupuncture and even the taste of chocolate (Eidelman et al. 2010). Sometimes it's easier to trust what's been around longer than take a risk for what we aren't sure is ahead. Or taking a risk at all.

One of my friends' favorite stops at any water park is always the lazy river. She'll just float along all day, letting the current take her where it will. On one of our trips, floating on the lazy river was so relaxing she fell asleep in the sun. We couldn't find her for quite a while; she was just aimlessly floating. She claims she's happiest when she can just sit back and coast—when she doesn't have to think much about which way to go.

Or take Alice, Lewis Carroll's curious heroine from her *Adventures in Wonderland*:

> Alice: Would you tell me, please, which way I ought to go from here?
>
> The Cheshire Cat: That depends a good deal on where you want to get to.
>
> Alice: I don't much care where—.
>
> The Cheshire Cat: Then it doesn't matter which way you go (1920, 89).

Indeed, not moving, changing, or proactively growing is a choice. In these cases, we are stuck—frozen—and don't thaw, never leaving space for change. The result of that choice can leave us living a life justifying the decisions made for us, perhaps without us even realizing it. The alternative allows us to be active participants in the process, continually thawing, changing, and refreezing.

Anna (whom we met earlier) was switched to a new team in her company's merger. The adjustment was rocky at first, and there were a lot of uncomfortable conversations as they navigated the transition. Her new manager consistently tried to push projects through before the entire review process was completed. Anna knew this wasn't good practice (or helpful to the team in the long run) and would try to speak up.

She was often shut down and once even told she should "stick to her job." But she continued to show up each day, doing what she did best. She would check in with her other teammates and build morale, continue to ask questions, and stay authentic to who she was and what she believed. Although it wasn't always comfortable, she often gently yet firmly ensured she needed the final review before anything was sent in for approval.

A few months later, her manager was let go, and Anna was offered his job. The new position was a huge promotion, and she doubted whether she was prepared to lead a team. Of course, she didn't have to accept the offer. She could stay where she was, doing exactly what she had been doing. But coasting along the lazy river wasn't something she wanted to do forever.

Anna was told her approach to collaboration, attention to detail, and leadership skills made her a clear candidate for the job. She wanted to believe she could do it—make the change—but the voices in her head were loud. She remembers the string of thoughts that ran through her head: "Everything in my mind screamed, 'Are you crazy? You're not qualified for this!'"

She recalls the moment she made her decision. She took a deep breath before she smiled and, with a confident handshake, accepted the position. Three years later, she became a top producer in her company. She began training others and speaking on best leadership practices at company events. When looking back on the decision she reflected, "I can't believe I even considered turning it down. At the time, it was just so hard to think about what would happen when things changed."

Further research on organizational change suggests one crucial reason resistance shows up is the threat of continuity to organizational identity (Venus et al. 2010). If we continue to apply what we learn from this research on organizations to our personal journey, we can ask a few important questions:

How can we ensure we won't lose the core of who we are when we change?

And if we don't have a choice and change is a part of our universal experience, how can we make it a little less daunting?

In 2020, after close to a decade of living in downtown Chicago, a global pandemic hit. Like most of the world, I went from living a whole, active, social existence to being isolated in complete lockdown. It gave me a lot of time to think, reflect, and wonder. *Why had I made the choices I made? What made me truly happy? What was keeping me here?*

When I thought about it, I realized the choice to move to Chicago in the first place might not have been totally of my own design. At the time, it had seemed like the right thing to do. Chicago is close to my family. I had a network and the prospect of a job. It's a great city. I had certainly made the most of my time there and created a world of opportunity for myself. But I craved more and wondered if it was time to make a change. I had the crazy thought maybe I would move, and start fresh in a new city.

My mind immediately flooded with all the reasons it wasn't a good idea. The dream wasn't probable or possible. I wasn't sure where to begin. Having created an entire life in Chicago,

I worried making a change would somehow devalue all the experiences I had or threaten the relationships I built. I had worked hard to create this life. *Did changing mean I had to lose something? What if there was more to gain by embracing whatever was ahead?*

Each individual's change journey is unique. But there are principles and tools we can invite into the experience of personal change. Values like curiosity, awareness, and non-judgment become guideposts for exploring concepts like stretch, permission, and perspective. When there are constantly more factors to consider, having a strong foundation becomes crucial for making intentional choices. Designing and building pathways to change—both now and forever—is a process that can be explored and embraced. These concepts may be simple, but they can offer powerful grounding for what can sometimes feel like an overwhelming prospect: change or be changed.

Famed drama critic Brooks Atkinson said, "The most fatal illusion is the settled point of view. Since life is growth and motion, a fixed point of view kills anybody who has one" (1951, 115). If we know we're in for a journey of change, perhaps we can start by considering what other illusions lay ahead and discover how we can tune in to (and perhaps begin to shift) our point of view. The process of change can be scary, but so is staying the same.

CHAPTER 2

The Illusion of Control

My first time in Las Vegas, a place where one stimulating experience followed the next, no matter where I looked, lights and sounds filled my senses. Tucked into my seat for the evening's show, I watched the excitement build around me as the heavy bass of loud music vibrated through my whole body. I finally caught a glimpse of the famous duo Siegfried & Roy. Performers of another caliber, their high energy (and a tiger!) made everything feel larger than life. They moved swiftly across the stage, their every gesture tracked with rapt attention. And then, it happened. Presto change-o. It was like nothing else I had ever seen.

I watched in awe as they made an elephant disappear. And as if that weren't enough, my jaw dropped in slow motion as the elephant magically appeared on the stage again. I sat utterly stunned. Frantic and scrambling, my brain tried to figure out how the feat was possible. I knew there had to be a trick. But at that moment, I didn't care. I flew to my feet along with 1,500 other audience members, joining in the thunderous applause.

Magic tricks captivate their audiences. We watch as, before our eyes, something disappears, materializes, or defies gravity. These feats challenge expectations of what we thought possible. Gustav Kuhn, author of *Experiencing the Impossible: The Science of Magic*, is also director of the MAGIC laboratory (Mind, Attention and General Illusory Cognition) in London, where the lens of magic is used to study a wide range of psychological questions around consciousness, attention, perception, magical beliefs, deception, and free will. In an article from the *Guardian* on what magic can reveal about how our brain works, Kuhn shares: "Magic relies on powerful psychological illusions and magicians create their tricks by exploiting gaps and errors in our conscious experience. [...] Our true perception is full of gaps and holes, and much more removed from reality than most of us imagine" (Kuhn 2019).

Kuhn's words deeply intrigued me. I've always been interested in neuroscience and psychology and fascinated by how the brain works. Knowing how powerful the brain is, it's easy to forget gaps in our perception can exist. Magic proves this. But how do these gaps affect our ability to change? Are there things we aren't even aware of that might hold us back? To navigate change, it becomes essential to shed light on our blind spots. In doing so, we illuminate obstacles in our path—some of which we may not even realize existed. Further exploration of these points of vulnerability and risk reveals six of the most significant barriers to change.

BARRIER #1: DECISION-MAKING MAY NOT WORK THE WAY WE THINK

There are more than a few misconceptions about how the brain works. Did you know when the lens in your eyes takes in an image, it's actually upside down and reversed? Or how about the fact that your brain makes decisions before you are consciously aware of them? Many people believe a decision to act produces an action as a result. Ruud Custers and Henk Aarts conclude in their research on the unconscious will that under some conditions, actions are initiated even though we are unconscious of the goals to be attained or their motivating effect on our behavior (2010).

A body of research in this field indicates, through the use of functional magnetic resonance imaging (fMRI) technology to track brain activity, we may not be as "in control" of our decision-making at the cognitive level as we think:

- Stefan Bode et al. conclude in their research that free decision-making tasks could be predicted up to ten seconds prior to conscious awareness (2011).

- Research from Roger Koenig-Robert and Joel Pearson at the University of New South Wales in Australia shows that a subject's choice of mental imagery could be decoded eleven seconds before the conscious decision was made (2019).

This also extends to what researchers consider "abstract choices"—decisions in which the response is not a simple binary of one or the other. In a study designed to measure the prediction of "free choices" for abstract intentions, subjects chose a task to perform as well as when to complete it. Results showed the brain started preparing for these voluntary actions up to a few seconds before a decision had even entered the subject's conscious awareness and could be predicted in brain activity four seconds before conscious decision-making (Soon et al. 2013).

The way we think our minds work, then, is a bit of an illusion. But if we don't make decisions in our conscious, thinking mind, where do we make them? Our subconscious often leads the way, coming online within and through our physical body. Spending most of our time in the world of thinking and logic, it's easy to forget the decision-making process isn't based solely in the mind. Of course this was true. How many times had I experienced it myself?

I remember a visit with a good friend I hadn't seen in a while. As soon as she opened the door, I could tell something was wrong. Although the words that came out of her mouth seemed perfectly on par with her normally chipper attitude, her body told a different story. Her shoulders were hunched over, and she nervously twirled her hair around her fingers while she spoke. After a few minutes of what felt like strained small talk, I could barely take it anymore.

"Hold on. Let's stop for a second. What's going on with you?"

"Nothing. I'm fine. Seriously." As she fidgeted with the ring on her left hand, I noticed her uneasy shifting. Her actions didn't seem to match her words.

"Seriously?" I asked.

She sighed as her head dropped and softly shook side to side. Everything wasn't okay. "I think I have to call off the wedding."

She went on to tell me that, although nothing in particular had happened, she had woken up for the past few weeks with a knot in her stomach. She tried to shake it off, and even started running again, thinking she just needed to clear her head. But ultimately, she knew continuing her engagement wasn't the right thing. I told her she needed to do what was right for her—there was no way she could go through with a wedding if this were how she was feeling.

She nodded and said quietly, "I think I've known for a long time. I just didn't realize it until now."

As difficult as it sometimes can be, we have to ask ourselves hard questions. Sometimes we might know the answers at the body level but are not yet fully aware in our mind. In my friend's case, her nagging sensations were her body's way of communicating with her. Tuning into—and honoring—the decisions made in our body system before we even realize them is an important part of getting out of our heads and breaking a significant barrier to change.

BARRIER #2: HABIT AND AUTOPILOT
I was eighteen when I first came to the Alexander Technique, and it was because of a jaw problem. I needed another solution to my situation to avoid an (overly aggressive) jaw surgery. Developed by Frederick Matthias Alexander in the late 1800s, the Alexander Technique is a process of psychophysical reeducation—the fancy term for mind-body. Based on a set of

guiding principles and accessed through physical exploration of the body system, lasting change can be discovered and sustained. Today, the Technique is utilized to help anyone do what they do better: with more ease, less effort, and more efficient results.

As my lessons continued week after week, I really wasn't sure how sitting in a chair, thinking about standing up, or pausing to give space before I took a step forward had *anything* to do with my jaw. It just seemed to be about exploring physical movements. But eventually, I realized it was about much more than positions and postures. Soon it became clear that even *thinking* about something caused a physical response in my body. My body habits were so strong, I didn't always consciously have a choice. This was what Alexander had discovered so many years before: the will to change a habit wasn't enough. If I stopped thinking about my choices before a new pattern was formed, the old habit would likely take over.

Our subconscious makes choices in how to move our bodies by leaning on these learned patterns—our habits. If I wanted to change these patterns, I had to find a path to leading the way more consciously. Otherwise, I realized I was just running on autopilot. Dr. Nicole LePera, author of *How to Do the Work: Recognize Your Patterns, Heal from Your Past, and Create Your Self*, says: "Our brain actually prefers to spend most of its time coasting on autopilot—it is best able to conserve its energy by knowing what to expect. This is why our habits and routines feel so comforting and why it's so unsettling and even exhausting when our routines are disrupted. The trouble is, following our conditioned routine keeps us stuck in that routine" (2019, 29).

We can get so comfortable and so stuck that changing these habits can actually feel *wrong*. So we can't always trust what is "comfortable." Different isn't always bad. It's just different. And ultimately, the entire thinking system needs to shift in order for us to truly change. As shown through various research on habit formation, simply deciding to "stop" isn't enough to make a habit or pattern disappear. We must create healthier, or perhaps more intentional, habits to take their place. This is another one of those instances where I'd love nothing more than to turn into a magician who can make bad habits disappear with the snap of a finger or the flick of a wand. But research on habit formation has shown, on average, it takes just over two months—sixty-six days—to create a new habit (Lally et al. 2009).

In his book *Atomic Habits: Tiny Changes, Remarkable Results*, James Clear comments on habit creation as a process: "All big things come from small beginnings. The seed of every habit is a single, tiny decision. But as that decision is repeated, a habit sprouts and grows stronger. Roots entrench themselves, and branches grow. The task of breaking a bad habit is like uprooting a mighty oak within us. And the task of building a good habit is like cultivating a delicate flower one day at a time" (2018, 22).

Successful habit creation begins with small acts repeated and reinforced so our system has the opportunity to integrate fully. Over time, as I studied (and eventually went on to teach) the Alexander Technique, my thinking habits changed. I didn't just stop to think about taking a step or choose how I wanted to sit down in a chair. I realized my entire approach to decision-making, choice, and change had shifted. Not just physical habits, but any habit could be shifted with this change in my thinking system and these principles.

So when it comes to habit and autopilot? Start small. Notice what you notice. Recognize that once you are aware, you can make a choice. Pause to ensure your system isn't just thinking (and deciding) on autopilot. Let go of judgment. Choose a different direction. Rinse and repeat.

BARRIER #3: THE PARADOX OF CHOICE

The more choices, the better, right?

The scene is familiar: It's been a long day, and I finally collapse on my comfortable couch, drink in one hand and a plate (okay, fine—a bowl) of salty snacks in the other. I'm ready to relax and unwind, so I call on my good friend, Netflix. I start scrolling as I think to myself, *What am I in the mood for?*

Already saw that one.

Not in the mood for an intense drama tonight.

Didn't my friend say this series was good?

Eh. I can't stand that actor.

Time goes by. Maybe it's five minutes, maybe close to an hour. I'm lost in the endless scroll of menu options and completely overwhelmed. I end up deciding to put on some music and clean out my closet instead. The "paradox of choice" says, while we might believe being presented with multiple options makes it easier to choose one we are happy with, having an abundance of possibilities actually requires more effort to make a decision and can leave us feeling unsatisfied with our choice (The Paradox of Choice 2022).

Consider the modern world of online dating. Whether you prefer Tinder, Hinge, Bumble, Match.com, OkCupid, or the newest app to hit the market, the process has come to resemble an addictive game that leaves many people feeling lonelier than when they started. Research shows "online daters who chose from a large set of potential partners (i.e., 24) were less satisfied with their choice than those who selected from a small set (i.e., 6). Those who selected from a large pool with the ability to reverse their choice were the least satisfied with their selected partner after one week" (D'Angelo and Toma 2016). We become less satisfied with the choices we make when there are more options to choose from.

Psychologist and author Barry Schwartz became interested in the fact that more choice was not only resulting in overload and paralysis but ultimately negatively affecting happiness. In his book *The Paradox of Choice: Why More Is Less*, he states: "Learning to choose is hard. Learning to choose well is harder. And learning to choose well in a world of unlimited possibilities is harder still, perhaps too hard" (Schwartz 2009, 75).

Ultimately, it's essential to understand more is not always better. I now keep a queue of shows and movies on my "to watch" list and set time parameters (and number limits) for swiping my way through dating apps. Although it doesn't eliminate the issue (or help me avoid bad dates), it certainly does help make the barrier a bit less daunting.

BARRIER #4: LIMITING BELIEFS AND TRIBAL SHAMING

I don't have time. I'm not qualified enough. Maybe she can, but I never could.

These are some of the limiting beliefs I have seen, felt, and painfully lived. They appear as absolute truths, stories I don't remember writing but somehow have shaped my decision-making. These thoughts don't make me want to leave my comfort zone, and they certainly make it seem like change is an impossible, scary prospect. The most challenging part about these limiting beliefs? Often we don't know they are there. These beliefs are subconscious. We may not even be aware of them until they are pointed out to us. Once we know, the choice of how to move forward becomes our own to make.

In the 2011 romantic sci-fi thriller *The Adjustment Bureau*, Matt Damon plays a young, up-and-coming politician. After a chance meeting with a dancer, everything changes. He feels compelled to follow her, deviating from his "intended" life path. That's when a group of men dressed in sunglasses and suits are tasked with restoring the problem—the glitch in the plan. Their purpose is to tidy up the lifelines of important people, making "adjustments" when they stray off course. Sometimes, our limiting beliefs can seem like this ominous group of men in suits trying to keep us on a narrow, limited path.

Harry, the sympathetic representative of The Adjustment Bureau assigned to make course adjustments, reflects: "Most people live life on the path we set for them, too afraid to explore any other. But once in a while, people like you come along who knock down all the obstacles we put in your way.

People who realize free will is a gift that you'll never know how to use until you fight for it" (Nolfi 2011, 1:38:35).

As much as we'd like to think we can do it all alone, the African proverb "It takes a village to raise a child" comes to mind. Community support is an incredibly important part of approaching any change. Sometimes it takes someone outside ourselves—a friend, family member, or professional—to help encourage us or point out our blind spots. Identifying these blind spots is an essential step in determining where to start. But when those around us question, challenge, or put down our plans to move forward, it can be a crushing experience.

Dr. Mario Martinez is a clinical neuropsychologist whose work explores how the immune system responds to cultural beliefs. Some of his work explores the topic of healing from tribal shaming. Our "tribe" is not just our family but our entire community, culture, and system of beliefs. In generations long past, sacred rules were established to preserve order and safety. Unspoken mandates required we live by these rules, as violating them could threaten both the health of the individual and the tribe. Those who broke these rules were often punished, and shame has long been a (very compelling) control tactic for keeping people in-line. Shame not only threatens our sense of connection and belonging but is also detrimental to our health.

Learning how your body responds to and holds beliefs is an aspect of change (and health) to attend to carefully. Martinez suggests honoring the truth of who (or what) needs to be abandoned for an individual to move forward and rebuild their strength. After all, if no one ever questioned or challenged beliefs, nothing would ever change. In his book *The MindBody Code: How to Change the Beliefs That Limit Your Health, Longevity, and Success*, Martinez shares: "True sustainable change requires gaining access to the cultural beliefs that deny you the rewards of your courageous commitment to change. It requires a new vision of how your body responds to your beliefs and how you can change those beliefs through an embodied approach" (2014, Intro).

No belief will be truly valid unless you fully embody it. Working with a somatic therapist or holistic practitioner can be a gateway to important learning—especially when we can't always see our blind spots. We can begin to release our limiting beliefs when we recognize we don't hold (or control) these beliefs in our brains and any shift, leap, change, or transformation becomes more possible when we reclaim our wholeness.

BARRIER #5: NEGATIVE BIAS

When David got called in for his first-year performance review, he was nervous. He knew he had done an excellent job quickly learning the ropes and worked with his team to fully integrate the company's new tech platform over the past six months. He had only met with his manager and her supervisor once—during his interview process—so he wasn't sure how the review would go.

They made him feel comfortable immediately and started sharing some of the great qualities he brought to the company as an employee and team player. They admired how quickly he had picked up new skills and commented on his creative eye, which helped see the project through to completion. And then they mentioned his occasional late arrivals to the office.

His heart sunk. Usually, he was just running a few minutes behind in the morning, but there was the occasional day he didn't manage to make it to his desk until after 9:15 a.m. He hadn't realized they noticed. They asked him to keep an eye on his arrival time and do his best to set an example for the other new employees, reiterating how glad they were to have him on the team. But when David's friends asked him how the review had gone, his response was: "Not great. I've been late and need to work on it." David had all but forgotten the other positive feedback they gave him in his review and instead was stuck on the one negative.

Dr. Rick Hanson, in his work on negativity bias, describes this phenomenon: "[Our brains are] like Velcro for bad experiences, but Teflon for positive ones" (n.d.). He shares that out of ten total experiences, just one negative experience changes our whole perception. We will often dwell on the negative. This comes from our biological evolution—we were wired to look out for the bad (dangerous) experiences as they could threaten our health, safety, and well-being. Current circumstances don't often require us to be very concerned with predators chasing us as we hunt for food, but this psychological phenomenon has still stuck. And it isn't helpful when it comes to navigating change. If anything, it prevents us from moving forward. Instead of two steps forward and one step back, negativity bias feels more like one step forward and nine steps back.

How do we counter this? We can begin by taking in more of the positives and reinforcing the good. With regular practice, we can work to intentionally wire in this habit. Sometimes this will require us to rewrite the stories we hear in our heads; stories with narratives focusing on the gaps in our knowledge and the things we didn't do. When we strengthen the ability to take in and reinforce the positives, we can begin to influence our next steps more actively.

BARRIER #6: FEAR AND TRAUMA
It was day two of a three-day virtual event—The Thriving Experience—where over a hundred women had gathered to learn from Dr. Valerie Rein, author of *Patriarchy Stress Disorder: The Invisible Inner Barrier to Women's Happiness and Fulfillment* and cocreator of The Thriving Method. As a psychologist and women's mental health expert, Dr. Rein works to help heal the individual, collective, and ancestral trauma pervasive in our world.

But I don't really have trauma. This was what popped into my head when I first came across her work and ideas. True, I had never had a significantly clinical, big-T traumatic event happen to me. But the way Rein went on to define trauma changed my perspective, striking a chord. She defines trauma as:

> *Any experience that made you feel unsafe in your fullest authentic expression and led to developing trauma adaptations to keep you safe* (2019, 18).

I now laugh at how naive I was to think I had never been made to feel less than, not good enough, or stifled for showing up fully. I recognize trauma is much more a universal experience than not. Rein's work, along with her partner Jeffrey Tambor's, establishes that creating a baseline of physical safety is crucial to healing. Their work utilizes somatic and energetic tools to heal trauma, building pathways to break away from simply surviving to live in a state of thriving.

One of her baseline somatic tools is called The Repower Tool. The simple act of feeling your feet on the ground, taking in your surroundings, activating the senses, and breathing does wonders to help reestablish a sense of presence and connection. Reorienting helps find and build safety. These early steps on the pathway to healing are important and crucial, and Rein shares: "When we see the invisible, we can do the impossible."

Where change is concerned, knowledge becomes a powerful tool. At the most basic level, these barriers reveal it's important not to bypass the intelligence of our bodies and live only in our heads. For most of us, it's a habit—an adaptation—to keep things living (and dwelling) in the mind because we think we have more control over what's happening that way. As we develop and practice ways to increase our awareness, we can begin to break that loop.

It has been said problems cannot be solved by the same level of thinking that created them. Increasing our awareness immediately shines a light into the dark spaces. As a first step, we establish a starting point and determine what we don't (yet) know. We illuminate blind spots we weren't aware of. This process helps discover the patterns, habits, and hurdles to change. Inevitable frustrations will arise as we stumble through periods in which things seem confusing. Sometimes discovering what we don't know can feel like getting hit by a ton of bricks.

It may be the way of human nature that we always end up drawn to things we don't completely understand. As Dr. Valerie Rein reminded me that day: "We have zero rational data points about the future." This is a very real fact. But perhaps by understanding just a little bit more about what is holding us back, the change process won't feel quite so daunting. All we can do is tackle the barriers one step at a time.

CHAPTER 3

Tools for Change

My friend's eleven-year-old son is obsessed with *Minecraft*. He thinks in the language of strategy and translates it into the game's blocky world where cities, homes, and farms (complete with pixelated, square animals) emerge. The game's simplistic visuals keep focus on the joy of constructing, deconstructing, and rebuilding again. He spends hours happily lost in exploring and creating, and it's often all he wants to talk about. (Although I don't fully understand most of our *Minecraft* conversations, I at least try to follow along.) One particular fall afternoon found us weaving through passersby along the sidewalk as we navigated the streets of the Upper West Side. Enthralled in his storytelling, my young friend repeatedly turned around to emphatically offer me gems from his trove of secrets. "And do you know what happens when you want to create a new place?"

I quickly zigged then zagged as I attempted to avoid errant dog droppings and dodge the occasional overly confident pigeon. "No, I'm not sure. I've never played *Minecraft*, remember?"

"Well, you go back to your inventory and see what tools you have. Then you can figure out how to build what you need.

And you gotta know whether you're in survival mode or creative. 'Cause that means you can do whatever. Got it?"

Not by a long shot. Confused, I tried to keep up. "Well, sort of. Tools? How do you get tools?"

"Oh, you know. Tools! Like stuff you use to mine things so you can build! Sometimes it takes a really long time because you have to make sure you have all the *right* tools. I mean, if you're trying to get diamonds, you need a diamond pickaxe. But if you're mining iron, then it won't work. You have to have the iron axe!"

Even with little to no knowledge of this game world, there was an important lesson here. No matter your interest, field, or area of expertise, it's essential to use the right tools. Collecting, building, and honing the right resources is a process. Knowing what tools to utilize (and what your inventory has in stock) is a learned skill. It might take time to develop, but it's crucial to moving forward. Even with consideration of the unexpected, tools help ensure there is a better baseline for maintaining balance as the next steps are taken.

Being adequately resourced is one of the most critical aspects of navigating change. It's tempting to think we need to turn outward or "mine" our world for tools we can use. But before looking for resources and tools we think we don't have, let's dig a little deeper into our own toolboxes. How deep? I'm talking about a bit of a dive. Underwater, in fact.

Along the seafloor in the pristine, blue coastal marine waters lives a creature who, for all intents and purposes, shouldn't last very long. A spineless invertebrate with no natural protection, she is more or less a liquid creature, much like the water she inhabits. Although susceptible to the hunters and other dangers of her natural environment, her ability to outwit and outthink her opponents makes her a fascination for the underworld (and the human mind).

She is an octopus. Her survival skills are the epitome of adaptability and resilience, and her intelligence sets her apart. Although unlike humans in many ways, she has undoubtedly mastered embodied cognition—an intelligence that lives not just in the brain but throughout the body. She exercises the skills to navigate her environment while keeping an incredible focus on the ability to respond to the now and remain prepared for what lies ahead.

This being in the present allows her to change instantly, whether expertly camouflaging herself to conceal from a predator or quickly inking an oncoming threat. Each of her eight tentacles houses a brain and, in conjunction with her main central brain, can make decisions. So, at first glance, it might seem her habit of collecting discarded shells, rocks, or even broken debris is haphazard. But she carefully washes each piece, and methodically uses them to close off the entrance to her carefully chosen cave or to traverse the ocean floor as if walking on stilts, to keep them with her in case they might come in handy in the future.

On full display are two essential tools for change: adaptability and resilience. According to Pew Research Center polls, these "tough-to-teach intangibles"—along with emotional intelligence, curiosity, and creativity—will be increasingly valued for learners in the twenty-first century (Rainie and Anderson 2017).

Adaptability can be defined as an *"appropriate cognitive, behavioral, and/or affective adjustment in the face of uncertainty and novelty"* (Martin et al. 2013).

Resilience is *"the power or ability of a material to return to its original form, [or] position [...] after being bent, compressed, or stretched; elasticity"* (Dictionary.com 2022).

The good news is we don't have to look far for these traits. We are hardwired to be adaptable and resilient. It's literally in our DNA; our entire sympathetic nervous system is designed with these built-in responses. We spring into action at the sight of a saber-toothed tiger charging our way (and run the other!). We freeze when we hear an unfamiliar sound and fight to protect ourselves at any cost. We all have these traits, although tapping into how best to use them more intentionally may vary for each individual. We may each be at various stages in our ability to lean into these tools, but they are never far.

Think about the first time you rode a bicycle. I'll bet there were a few cuts, scrapes, and bruises as you tried new things and still fell again and again. Until we figured out how to stay balanced, it was trial and error (combined with adaptation and resilience). By quickly learning from experience, we continued to get back up and try again until we could make it down the block. We lived for the moments when we could coast down the hill, the wind caressing our faces. With our hair blowing back, our timidly gripped hands would lift off the handlebars and spread out wide, fully embracing the ride. The thrill and rush of coasting weightlessly through the air traveled to the tips of our fingers.

Life offers us countless opportunities to hone these skills and develop resources around adaptability and resilience. One of my most memorable, and humbling, accounts of this process in action started in a way I wouldn't have predicted. The bright orange HOT YOGA letters on the outside of the building didn't leave any mystery why I was arriving at the studio early that morning. I stood at the counter of the extensive yet unpopulated lobby, waiting to check in. Wearing my cutest bold patterned workout clothes and holding my bright blue mat rolled up under my arm, I was a cocktail of excited, nervous, and scared.

After signing in, they gave me a quick tutorial on the clean, open space and told me where I could change, shower, and use the bathroom if needed. We then got to the details: The class was ninety minutes long, and the room would be heated to a temperature of 105 degrees. Since this was my first class, I should listen to the words, do my best, focus on breathing, and rest in a child's pose if I needed to. And, perhaps most importantly, try not to leave the room.

Got it. I wasn't new to yoga, so I wasn't exactly sure about all the fuss. I organized myself in the locker room and grabbed a quick sip of water. Instinctively, I paused for a moment before I opened the door and entered the hot room. I wasn't quite prepared as I crossed this threshold. The heat and humidity greeted me more like a solid brick wall than a gentle cloud of essential oils.

My body quickly got used to the heat (or so I thought). The first twenty (or so) minutes of the class weren't easy by any stretch, but they were manageable. I noticed my breathing was a little labored, and my body produced sweat in what seemed like solid sheets. Every time I wiped my forehead, a fresh coating would instantly appear. It wasn't exactly comfortable. There was no clock in the room, so I had no idea how long I had been in there. I just knew the whole experience became more and more difficult with each passing pose. My muscles were shaking. The sweat was still coming. No one else seemed to be struggling, so I tried to shake it off.

You can do this, Lisa. You can probably do this. Okay…just try to make it through.

And then camel pose came along. On my knees, I tipped my head back to look toward my feet, wondering if I had done it right. Unfortunately, there wasn't much time to dwell on the question. An unmistakable churning in my stomach sent me an obvious message. This wasn't going to end well. I suddenly realized if I didn't get out of the room quickly, it was likely to happen right there. I panicked—after all, we weren't supposed to leave the room!—but I couldn't take it anymore.

I frantically ran out of the room and straight into the bathroom, where I proceeded to throw up for the next few minutes. By the time the class had ended, I had barely regained my strength. I left in a hurry, mumbling an embarrassed apology to the teacher on my way out. I heard him say, "Try to stay in the room next time! I promise it will get better!"

Yeah, right.

I did go back again. (And ran out of the room to throw up when I got to camel pose for the second time.) Then I went back again. And again. My capacity for adaptability and resilience was stretched, not just because I adapted to the circumstances and environment. I also kept showing up and tapping in. Going back for a second, third, fourth, and eventually fortieth time. I was taking another step forward, even when I wasn't sure where it would lead me.

Soon the heat didn't feel that oppressive (on most days). Time spent in the hot room became a sanctuary for my busy brain. It took some time (and more than a few challenging classes), but after a while my breathing didn't labor (almost) at all. If you would have asked me at the end of that first day, there was no way I was *ever* going back. Years later, my ninety-minute moving meditation practice is still one of the few things that allows me to achieve a completely clear mind.

In hindsight, I realized I had to lose something very important to stay the course: judgment. I could have really beat myself down for running out of the room that first day. Hanging my head low, I could have vowed never to return. Instead, I chose to go back. Each time I made that choice, I wrote myself a different story.

Psychotherapist Esther Perel reminds us adaptability is "an essential part of resilience," "the conversation within us between stability and change," and "our ability to bend and come back to center over and over again, increasing our flexibility each time, whether we're in our daily stretch or the fight of our lives. And the more we practice becoming adaptable, the more we can tolerate change and harness its power" (Perel, n.d.).

Take a few lessons we can learn from ants. A 2016 research study on resilience in social infrastructure insect systems looked at how disruption affects the colony systems of ants. Three main areas of response to disruption demonstrated this concept of resilience: resistance, redirection, and reconstruction (Middleton and Latty, 2016). Some colonies invested in strong infrastructure, nests, and underground systems so they were highly resistant to disturbance. In the face of an impending threat, others could quickly redirect energy and resources. Their sense of pivoting focus allowed them to prevent the disturbance from being fatal. When neither of these options was possible, there was rebuilding in the aftermath—sometimes causing these systems to end up stronger than when they started. Some colonies used more than one of these response systems and even coordinated efforts to keep everyone thriving. But ultimately, the most important thing was the systems kept working. They didn't give up.

Adaptability and resilience are like muscles; traits that need to be strengthened, honed, practiced, and stretched. Eventually, they become incorporated into our thinking systems. We see how resilience shows up as we prepare for, respond to, and even rebuild again. We're not insects working to protect and preserve our colonies, but we are working to build and enhance our lives. Whether we study and rehearse our answers for a big interview ahead of time, navigate a board meeting by reading the room, or put the pieces back together after disappointment, the important part is we continue to show up.

Three crucial things come to light when utilizing these important tools for change. Leaning into these three "attitudes" will help us take steps toward achieving our goals:

1. **Observe (without judgment!):** Start by taking out the judgment. Take in your circumstances to learn more about them: The octopus doesn't concern herself with anything but what's in the present. This serves as a model. We can ruthlessly and cleverly use a combination of innate skills and the resources around us to support our process. Observation helps apply our tools. It asks us to look further and deeper and allows for shifts in our perspective.

2. **Respect the process:** Recognize change isn't always easy and is often a process. Although sometimes uncomfortable or unknown, each small opportunity to shift creates a stronger pathway forward. Stretching is an essential part of building strength and honing a skill, whether it's getting over a breakup, mastering a craft, or making it through your first hot yoga class.

3. **Don't be afraid to fall (or fail):** As Thomas Edison said, "I've tried everything. I have not failed. I have just found 10,000 ways that won't work" (Sarett 1983). Understanding what doesn't work and the lessons we can learn from things *not* working out can be supremely valuable to getting us to where we want to go.

Things may not always work on the first try, and sometimes we will need to tap into various layers of resilience to get us through. Take Michael Jordan: the six-time title winner and Hall of Fame basketball player missed over nine thousand shots in the course of his career. He lost almost three hundred games. To his own admission, he was trusted to take the game-winning shot twenty-six times and missed. On the surface of these statistics, he failed over and over again.

Facts, figures, or even results never tell the whole story. Although we don't know what it took for someone to get to where they are today, you can bet there was adaptability and resilience at play. Adapting happens every time you encounter a situation you haven't been in before and it stretches you in some way—be it a skill, an experience, or a tool. Resilience happens each time you fall (or fail) and try again.

Ultimately, that takes one more important tool for change: courage. Courage is a trait many of my friends and family have ascribed to me. I've always struggled to see myself that way. My brother-in-law is a firefighter who rushes into burning buildings and rescues people. *That* takes courage. But what I do know is I have done hard things. So many times those hard things have scared me, yet I've stayed the course. I've changed professional careers (a few times). I've learned new skills (recently took up Latin dancing). I've moved across the country to start a new chapter of life during a pandemic. And although I've had my heart broken too many times to count, I still walk into every first date with the hope *this time* it might work out.

Courage is defined by *Merriam-Webster.com Dictionary* (2023) as the "*mental or moral strength to venture, persevere, and withstand danger, fear, or difficulty.*" Courage greets us on the other side of venturing, persevering, and withstanding. I believe the sum of courage is more than its parts. It's what adaptability and resilience look like when married to an unrelenting commitment to stay true to who we are, no matter the circumstances. That authenticity creates a type of courage that is deeper and more vulnerable. In the words of Brené Brown, "Courage starts with showing up and letting ourselves be seen" (2013, 30). Showing up is important, but to move forward, we have to decide to start.

As we lean into courage, we discover it's not only a tool but also an essential companion on our journey. Similar to the other tools of adaptability and resilience, courage can be exercised (and strengthened) by regular use. Although there are many ways to describe and define courage, it's clear it doesn't mean waiting until you're completely ready (will we ever be?). It doesn't require showing up with full confidence to succeed. And it certainly is not about being (or even feeling) you are invincible. Courage is being afraid but still showing up, even if you aren't sure what the outcome will be.

If we can let go of predetermined outcomes, we can remain open to all the ways courage reveals itself. Mary Anne Radmacher, in her book *Courage Doesn't Always Roar*, wisely reminds us, "Courage does not always roar. Sometimes courage is the quiet voice at the end of the day that says, 'I will try again tomorrow'" (2009). And sometimes, that's enough.

Change is rarely (if ever) linear. If we want to navigate a path that isn't straight, our tools need to be flexible. These three tools—adaptability, resiliency, and courage—give us an "ARC" that allows us to move into change armed to take on whatever lies ahead. They are tools we can carry with us and use to help design our emerging realities. They don't order neatly in a straight line but follow a flexible, moveable path.

In the rest of my unexpectedly wise conversation on the sidewalks of New York, I did also find out *Minecraft* allows you to choose a game mode to play in: two options being survival and creative modes. In survival mode, resources are limited, and players work to stay alive in a world with rules generated by someone else. But in creative mode, there is unrestricted potential for imagination, application of resources, and the ability to build. Creative mode allows you the freedom to choose your own adventure, architecting the world in which you want to live. I doubt I'll ever spend my free time playing *Minecraft*. But I do know I want to design and build in creative mode in my life.

CHAPTER 4

Into the Unknown

The credits had rolled, and the screen had gone black. The ushers had already come in to sweep up errant pieces of popcorn off the floor. I was grateful for the darkness of the room. My eyes were raw from crying, and every inch of the one or two tissues I happened to have in my bag had been used. The bottom half of my sleeves had become moist casualties of the emotional response to what I had just seen. This Disney movie had struck a chord, stirring something deep within me.

While *Frozen II* had all the makings of a successful family animation flick—catchy songs interwoven through stories of family, friendship, and a heroic journey to save a beloved kingdom—it was so much more than that. It was a story of change, transformation, and evolution. There was the knowing, urging pull for Elsa to follow her inner voice even when she wasn't sure what was ahead. Then came the discovery that the tools she needed had already been inside her the whole time, and *she* might have been the one she had been waiting for. (Sob.) Perhaps the biggest takeaway from this story was the messaging around what to do when you don't know what to do.

The advice? Just do the next right thing. Take a step, and then step again. A grief-stricken Anna reflects that looking too far ahead is overwhelming. Her sister Elsa had carelessly gone "too far" to find the truth and was gone. People were trapped in an enchanted forest. She needed to save her kingdom. All she could do was focus on the next right thing: one breath, one step, and the next right choice. Seeing only a sliver of light, she was unsure what was on the other side. The next right thing meant moving into the unknown, even through fear.

American author H.P. Lovecraft wrote: "The oldest and strongest emotion of mankind is fear, and the oldest and strongest kind of fear is fear of the unknown" (2013, 1). Psychologically defined, an unknown is the perceived absence of information at any level of consciousness. Scientific evidence offers reasons to believe that fear of the unknown is a fundamental and universal fear (Carleton 2016a). We know it as the involuntary response of our sympathetic nervous system: fight, flight, or freeze. Biologically, we are wired to respond to any stimulus in our environment that might threaten our safety. Our autonomic nervous system response is rigid, automatic, and hypervigilant, "designed to maximize safety and minimize danger" (Carleton 2016b).

Venturing into the unknown can feel like walking to the edge of a cliff without knowing how to get across. On top of fear, this can lead to emotions such as uncertainty and anxiety related to our lack of knowledge about what lies ahead (whatever that may be). These emotions are big, scary, overwhelming, and very real. Often, we are left unsure of what to do or how to move forward.

Considering this predicament brought me back to the first time I came across Chip Conley's book *Emotional Equations*. The premise made so much sense: emotions can be broken down into mathematical equations. By considering the building blocks of emotions—the parts that create them—he provides insights into their contributing factors. Armed with a conscious awareness of the pieces that create our emotions, we can shine a light on how it may be possible to shift them and make changes. In a *Forbes* interview about his book, Conley shares: "The more we are conscious about what creates Regret or Envy, the more we can influence those ingredients and have some emotional mastery in our lives" (Schawbel 2012).

Our experiences are never one-dimensional. But considering emotional equations is a valuable tool. Rewriting these big, difficult emotions allows me to see them differently. Dissecting anxiety, one of the more complex emotional equations we face in life, we discover it can be broken down. Anxiety is made up of two contributing parts: uncertainty and powerlessness (Conley 2012, 80). Combined, these are potent factors that create a more challenging sum than their parts.

I'll never forget the look in one of my good friends' eyes when she told me she was pregnant. She was in her early twenties and hadn't been married very long. The pregnancy wasn't "planned." Of course, they wanted kids; they just hadn't expected it to happen so soon. She was a mix of emotions. She was absolutely thrilled at the prospect of welcoming a little one into the world. Full of awe, she realized she could finally create the family she had always dreamed of. She was also aware she didn't know what she was doing. Fear overwhelmed her.

Maybe she wasn't ready to be a mom. Uncertainty about what would happen to her body, life, and career filled her mind.

Although there weren't yet visible signs of this impending change, speaking it out loud seemed to make it even more real. Her hand tenderly fell to her lower stomach, resting gently as she closed her eyes. A few heavy tears fell, trailing down her slightly reddened cheeks. At that moment, the combination of uncertainty and powerlessness I sensed was honest, strong, and valid.

She took a deep breath. "It's going to be okay, right?"

"It's going to be more than okay. You're going to be such an amazing mom." As I hugged her, I could feel her body soften.

"I know." The edges of her lips curled into a soft smile. "It's pretty amazing, huh?"

It's easy to look back and forget how much happens in small moments where we can identify the emotions accompanying change. My friend felt immense fear and intense anxiety over the uncertainty and powerlessness of an unknown future. This change was permanent. Having no rational data points on what life would look like in seven short months was an uncomfortable feeling. Unsure of whether she even had all the skills for this new job, she felt frozen in her tracks.

With 20/20 vision, our hindsight is clear. Sometimes we may even laugh when we consider our reactions to certain situations. After all, reaction itself is a natural process, albeit a somewhat habitual one. Conley points out, "The truth is that most of us are very reactive with our emotions, but we aren't always conscious of that. Yet, what we're unconscious of often holds power over us" (Schawbel 2012).

It's an intense struggle to predict a future we have very little information about. Becoming conscious of our emotions and taking the time to reorient to our current situation can help us escape the loop fear and anxiety create. This "great unknown" can feel like coming up to the edge of that cliff, our feet frozen and planted. Looking out over the vast divide in front of us can make the journey ahead feel insurmountable.

There's a very explainable reason for this. In her book *How Emotions Are Made: The Secret Life of the Brain*, psychologist Dr. Lisa Feldman Barrett outlines her Theory of Constructed Emotion, which incorporates social, psychological, and neurological elements. Emotions aren't responses to something that happens, the way we might think. Rather, our brain combines concepts, information about system regulation, and experience to *make* emotions.

Our brains are like architects who create scaffolding using data from the past. And the process of prediction is precisely what happens in an ongoing loop. The brain makes a prediction which becomes a simulation. These simulations are compared with actual data from our sensory input. If they match, the prediction becomes our experience. If not, our brain will go back and work to resolve the errors by making another prediction (Barrett 2017, 63).

Emotions are made partially to keep our systems regulated—to keep our body budgets balanced—but they are also communicators of meaning. Emotions explain physiological shifts and feelings within our system, helping us make sense of the changes around us.

The fable of "The Donkey in the Well" (n.d.) explains these principles in action:

> *One day a farmer's donkey fell down into a well that the farmer had accidentally left uncovered. The animal cried piteously for hours as the farmer tried to figure out what to do. Finally, he decided the animal was old, and the well needed to be covered up anyway, so it just wasn't worth it to retrieve the donkey.*
>
> *He invited all his neighbors to come over and help him. They all grabbed a shovel and began to shovel dirt into the well. At first, the donkey realized what was happening and cried horribly. Then, to everyone's amazement he quieted down.*
>
> *A few shovel loads later, the farmer finally looked down the well. He was astonished at what he saw. With each shovel of dirt that hit his back, the donkey was doing something amazing. He would shake it off and take a step up.*
>
> *As the farmer's neighbors continued to shovel dirt on top of the animal, he would shake it off and take a step up. Pretty soon, everyone was amazed as the donkey stepped up over the edge of the well and happily trotted off!*

There's a reason this story isn't called "The Farmer and his Donkey." This is a story of finding yourself in the shoes of the donkey: scared, uncomfortable, and perhaps even stuck. Sometimes it feels like the world around you is tossing dirt in your path rather than creating a way to support and encourage change. On the surface, it seems all could be lost. Neither the facts nor the predictions look good. The pathway isn't yet carved out, and we can't see what's next. There doesn't seem to be a way out, up, or even through.

I was out celebrating my friend's birthday when I received the news of my mom's breast cancer diagnosis. The "three to five business days" waiting for results from the biopsy were painfully long, yet the doctors had been fairly blunt. "Didn't look good," "Very suspect," and "You should prepare yourself for a diagnosis" were all phrases my mom had heard that week. So when the text came through to call her, I immediately excused myself to do just that.

She answered on the first ring. "Well, it's cancer."

Given the ominous warning, maybe I had suspected this result, at some level. But it didn't soften the blow.

As we continued talking, she explained what she knew and the basics of the next steps. She had already spoken to my brothers and sister and had even gotten ahold of my sister-in-law and her grandsons in Japan. I sensed her diagnosis became more real with each share. We knew she'd have an appointment the following week, and until then, the plan was to take things one step at a time. All things considered, she sounded okay. I marveled at her strength and courage to hold it together when so much was still unknown.

I told her I loved her and hung up the phone, my hands still slightly shaky from the conversation. My mind rolled through memories of my childhood. I couldn't remember my mom ever being sick. In fact, she was always the one taking care of other people. The whole thing didn't seem real, right, or fair. *Was this really happening?*

I couldn't move for a minute. Our conversation continued to echo in my head, not quite finding a stable place to land. I was trying to focus on her and what she needed. But I wasn't even sure what my next step was. To be honest, I felt a bit like the donkey.

Anxiety and fear are two of the most challenging emotional barriers to the process of change. Tossing in the other pieces of the anxiety equation—uncertainty and powerlessness—leaves quite a bit of emotional charge to contend with. These barriers make us feel like we are stumbling around in the dark, afraid to move for fear of what might result from one misstep.

Although I wasn't sure what to do, I knew I needed to start by stopping. I checked in to see what was happening in my body. Internally, I could feel all those emotions bubbling up. Instead of just avoiding what seemed inevitable, I wondered what would happen if I tried to make friends with these unwelcome guests.

Standing there in the hallway, I noticed how fear showed up. I found myself a little frozen. My shoulders were practically living up in my ears. I had also been holding my breath. My tightened jaw was gripping hard. Anxiety might be the presence of powerlessness and uncertainty, but it also showed up in my body as my heart racing, my shoulders tensing, and a slight shaking as I paced. I took a deep breath. I didn't know what else to do next. Tears welled up, yet, at that moment, some of my fear and anxiety started to melt away.

Returning to Dr. Barrett's research, I was reminded emotions are created partially to reregulate our internal system. We can develop new concepts and emotions by having (and reinforcing) new experiences. In doing so, we expand and improve our system's predictive ability and generate different future responses to change. This translates to both changes in our environment and within ourselves.

It can be hard to move in the well of anxiety and fear. But by stopping to allow space, an opportunity for something new arises. Emphasizing a moment-to-moment awareness of internal and external events and calling on nonjudgmental acceptance can help eliminate anxiety about a future that is often unknown. Research by Dan Grupe and Jack Nitschke on uncertainty and anticipation in anxiety suggests this can be done by incorporating mindfulness techniques (2013). As you may have guessed, many mindfulness practices start with a focus on the breath.

In *The Big Leap*, Gay Hendricks offers insights on what he calls "the way through." He shares that the same mechanisms that create excitement also create fear. "There's only one way to get through the fog of fear, and that's to transform it into the clarity of exhilaration." Excitement and fear are two sides of the same coin. But excitement is fueled by breath, and fear develops quickly when we *hold* our breath. Hendricks suggests leaning into the fear instead of ignoring it and celebrating it as if blowing out the candles on a birthday cake. "Do that, and your fear turns into excitement. Do it more and your excitement turns into exhilaration" (Hendricks 2009, 18).

We may not be able to change our physical circumstances at any moment, but we do always have the ability to check in with what's happening in our body system. Simply stopping, feeling the ground under our feet, and taking a breath can allow us to reorient and take the next step. Perhaps we may even begin to transform the fear into exhilaration. Staying present and focusing on where you are in a particular moment (without judgment) is always a choice. Iconic *Grey's Anatomy* character Dr. Cristina Yang elaborates on this paradox in her own moment of stepping into the unknown: "Sometimes the future changes quickly and completely, and we're left with only the choice of what to do next. We can choose to be afraid of it. Just stand there trembling, not moving. Assuming the worst that can happen. Or we step forward into the unknown and assume it will be brilliant" (D'Elia and Pelan 2014). We can always make choices about when, and how, to move forward.

Growing up with nursery rhymes, I was familiar with good old Humpty Dumpty. In his children's book *After the Fall*, Dan Santat reveals the story we may not have heard—how Humpty Dumpty got back up again. Humpty, after being put back together again, is, well, traumatized. He is also afraid of heights. This is problematic, considering the top of the wall he once enjoyed requires climbing up a tall ladder. Patched together (by all the king's men), he cautiously approaches the world. Although he misses his perch and the view from above, he ultimately decides he'll have to find another way to connect to the big world.

He works tirelessly to design the perfect paper airplane that will allow him to experience the view from the big sky above without taking the risk himself. Then one day, his plane flies over the wall. The only way to get it back is to climb up to the top of the wall—the site of his great fall—again. He almost walks away. Instead, he chooses to make the climb. Terrified, he starts. He doesn't look up. He doesn't look down. He just climbs the ladder. Step by step, he ascends each rung until, eventually, he reaches the top. Finally ready to crack out of his shell, he sheds what he no longer needs and soars.

The unknown is most certainly just that. Unknown. But what do we risk if we don't try? T.S. Eliot's very *Frozen II* appropriate quote comes to mind: "'Only those who will risk going too far can possibly find out how far one can go" (Eliot, 1931).

At this point in my life, I've watched *Frozen II* no less than a dozen times. Anna emerges from the cave and listens to her gut—that inner voice—as she continues to do the next right thing. She makes choices that honor herself and the truth, even if she risks ruining her kingdom in its wake. Ultimately, the story has a happy ending. The fog is lifted from the enchanted forest, and everyone ends up exactly where they need to be. At the end of the movie, the naively innocent yet supremely observant snowman, Olaf, reflects that enchanted forests are places of transformation, and everyone comes away changed. *Frozen II* codirector Chris Buck elaborates on this concept in an interview where he shares, "They're a metaphor for life, and change comes for you whether you like it or not. And sometimes all you have is yourself" (Topel 2019).

Ultimately, it's not whether choices are right or wrong. It's just about making them. I believe no step is wrong if it moves you. In fact, as author and pastor Naeem Callaway reminds us: "Sometimes the smallest step in the right direction ends up being the biggest step of your life. Tiptoe if you must, but take a step" (Callaway, n.d.). And we watch as the unknown unfolds:

My friend became an incredible mother. Today, she has four amazing kids.

The donkey made it out of the well, and I hope he kicked the farmer for trying to leave him down there!

Humpty Dumpty conquered his fears and finally soared.

Together Anna and Elsa save the day—again!

I wish I could tell you I knew with certainty how my mom's story would play out in the long run. I don't. Some life changes are permanently altering and won't ever have a distinct endpoint. The unknowns will keep coming. Even with two successful surgeries behind her, there's always a risk, and continued fear and anxiety. With cancer, each appointment, procedure, check, and recheck can feel like walking right up to the edge of that cliff.

Each time there's more information, a new pathway reveals itself as the next right thing. We recognize and honor emotions, primarily related to the unknown, that arise. We do what we can to take things one step at a time, even if that means just stopping for a moment and letting our system reregulate. We can reorient and move forward with just a little less fear.

There isn't an owner's manual for change—or for being human, for that matter. I wish there were. I am consistently reminded that change, although complex, is inevitable. But there is comfort in the reminder that venturing out into the unknown is never the end of the story.

PART II

CHANGING NOW

"The secret of change is to focus all of your energy, not on fighting the old, but on building the new."

—SOCRATES, *WAY OF THE PEACEFUL WARRIOR*
BY DAN MILLMAN

CHAPTER 5

Caution: Change in Progress

Growing up, the first day of school was one of my favorite days. After a summer spent mostly reading, taking in baseball games, riding bikes, and playing with the kids in the neighborhood, I couldn't wait to meet my new teacher and classmates. A new classroom always seemed to invite the promise of "more." I'd hunt for the laminated name tag taped to the corner of the brown desk where I could claim my space for the next school year.

I'd carefully lift open the lid and unpack my new school supplies. The crayons, pencils, colorful notebooks, and folders were all carefully placed, ready to be called upon at a moment's notice. My desk was like a sacred space that served as an anchor for what inevitably became another year of learning and growth. It housed collections of the pages I read and the worksheets where I practiced honing my skills. The edges of notebooks were decorated with drawings and doodles. It was a treasure chest where I could track my progress and cultivate my dreams.

In hindsight, I can look back and chart the years I grew an inch or two (although after an early height peak, I'm now often one of the shorter people in the room). There were seasons of growth when I learned a new skill. Years came and went, as did friendships. I experienced things for the first time. I was ready to be shaped, molded, and moved toward whatever was ahead. In many of those moments, I was ripe for change.

As an adult, moving toward change can feel less comfortable than the predictable back-to-school routine. No longer in the pool's shallow end, we're reminded our feet can't always touch the ground. Treading water, we must decide in which direction we will swim next. Eventually, leaving the comfort of our homes, we may find ourselves standing in the middle of a big city, staring at skyscrapers looming high above. Sometimes it's overwhelming. We might feel lost or a bit disoriented.

How do we begin?

Where do we begin?

What can ultimately help us move forward?

A vision. In Roy T. Bennett's *The Light in the Heart*, he suggests: "Create a vision for the life you really want and then work relentlessly toward making it a reality" (Bennett 2020, 90). When we are armed with vision and intention, we have a baseline, a compass, and a North Star. We can work to make sure the conditions are right. Gathering the appropriate tools, we orient ourselves in the right direction. We look out for barriers and blind spots that might hold us back. We do the next right thing. We take the next steps forward and remember change is a work in progress.

At twenty-nine, Joseph was a successful professional. He had a solid medical device sales job that earned him enough to live well and have some fun too. He traveled, played golf, and generally enjoyed his life and free time. But he felt a nudging that became more and more pervasive. As he went to hospitals and met with doctors, he realized something didn't fit. After a while, he understood he didn't just want to interact with doctors as a salesman. He wanted to *be* a doctor.

Starting the path to becoming a doctor at age twenty-nine isn't exactly how most enter the profession. He'd have to go to medical school, of course. Following, he'd have years of residency and fellowship. All relatively predictable steps. But he didn't have an undergraduate degree with enough relevant courses to pursue this track. This meant he would have to complete a two-year post-bachelor, pre-graduate program to even *apply* to medical school. The hard facts of the journey ahead became clear:

- He'd be looking at a minimum of ten to twelve years of school, more if he decided on a surgical residency.
- The cost of this schooling would mean quite a hefty sum, carried in student loans.
- He would be almost a decade older than his other colleagues by the time he started medical school.

The long and short of it: moving forward with this vision would ultimately change not only his immediate course but also his entire life. For him, there wasn't a question about whether to move forward. So he rolled up his sleeves and got to work on making his vision a reality. This required change.

Hearing Joseph's story wasn't the first time I encountered what I now recognize as a defining moment in the change process. Even in my own experiences, I have often come up against these intersections of change. With the familiar push, pull, and sometimes even fear came a deep knowing that once the choice had been made, it was no longer a matter of when but how.

I could tell you my decision to move across the country to New York City and start a new chapter of my life in my late thirties hinged on several things falling into place. Or writing a book on change was something I just woke up one day and decided to try. The reality was I had been thinking about these things for years. Ideas quietly simmering on the back burner seemed to be biding their time until all the ingredients had blended just right. Perhaps without realizing it, I had been laying a foundation and preparing myself for the potential of action for some time.

Our change process can start by gathering all the ingredients for the perfect meal, collecting supplies, and organizing our desks on the first day of school. But eventually, dreams must move into reality. Preparation is readied for action. We take our vision and turn it into a job site—a construction zone—where change is actively in progress. Utilizing the right approach, creating optimal conditions, gathering supplies, and putting supports in place allows us to architect our vision. Bringing this vision to life requires a few important steps:

MOVE THE VISION INTO ACTION

We spend time dreaming, ideating, and creating blueprints. Drafting plans, we begin to architect our vision. As we discuss and share it, we get more excited about how our vision might become a reality. In my own experience, I had been thinking about writing a book for years. I'd sit down to write, get a few pages in, and think, *What am I doing?*

I'd put it away and forget about it until I got the itch to write again. This cycle continued until I decided I would set a goal to start working on this book. It still felt like a bit of a dream, to be honest. I knew what I wanted to write about—I had the vision—but I had no clue where to start. For me, the pathway came in the form of a writing course being offered. I knew it was my chance, so I jumped in. Although I wasn't entirely sure how everything would come together, I took the critical step of making a choice. I put on my hard hat and fiercely committed to bringing my vision to life.

It can be easy to dream. But I'm reminded of Napoleon Hill's famous quote: "A goal is a dream with a deadline" (Farber 2003, 60). Rather than getting caught in a loop of thinking, considering, wondering, second-guessing, and nonaction, we must ultimately choose in order to allow change to arise. This moves us from a passive to a more active role in the process of changing.

SURVEY THE ENVIRONMENT

Working to establish a strong foundation, we research, gather information, apply for permits, and check the city code. We set up a protected area to preserve and support our growth and development. With an understanding of some of the challenges and conditions we might be presented with, we can think ahead. We plan. Continuously, we make choices that will inform our next direction.

In Joseph's story, this step was crucial in moving him forward. Surveying his environment was the first step in laying the groundwork for his intended changes, and discernment was required. Classes had to be carefully chosen. It was essential tracked courses were taken in the correct order and all prerequisites were met. He also had to protect the ability to enact his plan by making clear and intentional decisions. These included moving closer to his school and into a smaller apartment and adjusting his budget and spending to live like a student. Social time had to give way to studying, and priorities had to be checked.

As he continued to clear away the excess debris and survey the conditions, he readied his site for change. We can do the same. Choices are made, helping us determine what is (and is not) needed. Pieces are slowly put in place, one decision at a time. The direction of our vision is further honed, and we are propelled forward.

BRING IN THE RIGHT TOOLS

Laying the further groundwork for growth and change requires tools. We begin to seek out the various resources we'll need to support us. We build scaffolding. Enacting our plans and dreams may necessitate finding and bringing in the right equipment. As we employ our resources, we may need to consult experts to help optimize our outcome.

In the initial years I studied and trained to become a teacher of the Alexander Technique, I was introduced to foundational principles of change that became essential tools to navigate the process of changing. Looking at any system, problem, or situation as a holistic structure, I utilized awareness, inhibition (pausing), recognizing habit, intentional direction, and considering the "how" of the process—often more than the end goal. Developing these tools allowed me to learn to speak the language of change. I was able to use these understandings to alter the way change showed up in my life, first in my physical body movements. Eventually, I applied this language of change in my approach to the world. Once fluent, I could translate this knowledge to any situation.

Adding in the other important internal tools for change—including adaptability, resilience, and courage—can help our actions shift from habit and solidify into intention. The relationship between intention and behavior change is important to consider. Research from Thomas Webb and Paschal Sheeran indicates the more significant our change in intention, the stronger the resulting action (2006). Knowing we have autonomy over our ability to influence a course of action empowers us to respond. Keeping our vision in mind, we chart a plan. Rather than simply reacting, we respond with intention and get to work.

CHANGE IN PROGRESS

When we break it down, there are three crucial skills and resources for moving change forward that can be used to support and encourage our process. As they interact, they help grow, expand, and optimize how change emerges. These components are:

- Stretch
- Permission
- Perspective

Stretch is essential for change, and permission and perspective act as levers that increase choice and opportunity. Over the following few chapters, we'll explore these components in greater depth to understand how they can be leveraged, embraced, utilized, and applied to change.

MAKE ADJUSTMENTS AS NECESSARY

The construction zone of change is truly a work in progress. Although it may be tempting to think of a "zone" as something fixed, concrete, and predictable, it's not. And that's *good*. Because neither are we. We are constantly shifting and changing, so the idea of a zone that adjusts and adapts with us is not only a relief but also works to our benefit.

Susan Froemke's documentary *The Opera House* chronicle's the construction of the iconic Metropolitan Opera in its current home in New York City's Lincoln Center. Since its opening in 1966, countless operagoers, passersby, and tourists have been inspired by its majestic landscape. Adorned with crystal starburst chandeliers, rich burgundy, and larger-than-life art, the Metropolitan Opera's home is the epitome of glamour. But it went through no less than forty-four versions before it came to life as it stands in Lincoln Center today. Architect Wallace K. Harrison, who had designed both Rockefeller Center and the United Nations, needed to continuously alter his design to fit budget, space, and vision constraints (Peers 2018). The final version incorporated elements not even considered in its original plans.

There is no shame in honoring and embracing the parts of our lives that are under construction. Our initial vision of a massive skyscraper might turn into a more modern office building better suited to its environment. Rather than a new building, we might realize we need to construct a bridge or a tunnel that connects us to our next step. Or it may be our structure is actually in great shape, just in need of renovation.

No matter what we are trying to create, it doesn't happen by snapping our fingers. Collecting all the right pieces of the puzzle is important, but so is stepping back and making adjustments so we stay on course. Anyone who has been through a renovation of any kind knows staying on time and on budget can be challenging. As we take time to look at the details of any job site, and our vision, we architect its progress and determine what is needed to get us over the finish line. The result almost always emerges as more than the sum of its parts.

Joseph went on to tirelessly commit to his vision over the next decade of his life and works as a medical doctor today.

Me? I made the move to New York City. And here you are, reading this book.

Change is possible. Often, change is already in progress.

CHAPTER 6

Step Into Stretch

It was a beautiful day for a ball game. A large part of our summer family time was spent out at the ballpark, a minor league stadium not far from where we lived. Piling in the car to head to the field was one of my favorite things. Without fail, I was greeted by an array of sights, sounds, and smells that transported me to another world. Surrounded by the endless hustle and bustle of fans, exuberant cheers exploded across the stands as a home run soared high over the center field fence. To this day, a baseball stadium remains the only place (in the world) that makes me crave a hot dog.

I loved speaking the language of the game. Settling in with my score sheet felt like arriving somewhere familiar. I'd keep the score, pitch by pitch, charting each play. To an outsider, the combination of numbers, letters, and lines on the page might look like sports hieroglyphics. To me, they offered a path to telling the story of what happened on the field that day.

Watching the pitchers was always my favorite. I was fascinated with how their graceful windup motion ushered the action to life. In one game, I noticed something shift after the opposing team got a man on base. The pitcher changed his stance. Inquisitively, I turned to look at my dad. The bright sun caused one of my eyes to reflexively squeeze shut as I asked him, "What's he doing that for?"

Without moving his gaze from the action, he explained, "He's pitching from the stretch."

"Why?"

"Well, the situation changed. Now there's a runner on base he has to watch out for. He'll be able to respond quicker—have a chance to catch him if he tries to steal the base."

Another delivery tactic had strategically replaced the regular, extended rhythm of the pitcher's windup. A change in the circumstances caused him to adjust and shift his approach. Utilizing this "stretch" created a different opportunity to influence the course of the game, one batter at a time.

Stretch is not just useful for athletes or a term we often associate with strengthening our muscles. It's a place where we can learn, grow, and, ultimately, change.

Karl Rohnke, known for his work in experiential education, applied a model for change based on the Yerkes-Dodson law. Robert M. Yerkes and John D. Dodson discovered a relationship between performance and stress—a moderate amount of stress applied would increase performance, but only up to a certain point (1908). A bit of a "Goldilocks" principle in action. Rohnke sets up the Comfort, Stretch, Panic model, which can be applied to help us understand how to maximize stretch as applied to change:

- In a state of Comfort, we live amid routine, habit, and predictable patterns. Comfort is safe, reassuring, and often calm. We can be moving on autopilot or engaging in a way that supports what we need but doesn't ask much of us. Usually, we are reasonably confident of what we can achieve in this space, but over time we can become bored, disengaged, or have the feeling we are static.

- In Stretch, we are challenged, pushed, and tested. We are asked to expand, assimilate, engage, and learn outside our comfort zone. Much like the word implies, boundaries are expanded. Stretch takes us further than we might be comfortable and is often new and unfamiliar. But with a "Goldilocks" amount of pressure, we can attain new skills and expand our potential. This can alter our course in a moment and affect our end trajectory where change is concerned.

- In Panic, our system becomes overloaded with stress. A sympathetic nervous system response takes over, and we are thrown into a state of fight, flight, or freeze. Primarily concerned with reestablishing safety within the system, performance decreases. Brain and body focus shifts to more important biological balancing factors. As a result, we often cannot perform, much less make changes. Our body is focused on simply surviving.

To optimize growth, we must be aware of our edges. Encouragement out of our comfort zone leads to stretch, but too far and we can land in a panicked mode. What does it look like to explore this concept in action?

Before training for her first marathon, Jacqueline only ran about eight miles consecutively. She could accomplish this fairly easily and without much effort. She had her usual route and routine and always felt great when she finished. It was the perfect amount of time for her to catch up on an audiobook or podcast, and she came home tired but energized and ready to tackle her next task. This was her comfort zone. She knew if she were to wake up and try to run the 26.2 miles of a marathon the next day, it would throw her body into panic mode. Her stamina couldn't manage, let alone her muscles and joints.

Her training process, which took place over about twelve weeks, laid out a daily plan for how far to run. It also accounted for rest days and more leisurely runs. Sometimes, she would only run a few miles. Inevitably, each time she got to one of the "longer" runs, she would start to feel stretched. Getting winded, she'd check her Garmin and routinely see she still had two miles left. Panic was the first thing that popped into her mind. She wasn't sure she could make it.

She'd consider stopping, but that didn't feel like what she needed. She would close her eyes and take a few deeper breaths, reconnecting to the sound of her feet rhythmically hitting the pavement. She'd remind herself she could always walk for a bit if she had to. Inevitably, she'd realize the two miles left were closer to one—something she knew she could tackle easily. With each long run after long run, she'd repeatedly accomplish her goals. Little by little, she stretched herself.

To stretch, she had to understand (and respect) her comfort edges. Leaning into them allowed her to make a choice to step into the space of being challenged and stretched. Although no semblance of a runner myself, I've cheered friends on through their journeys to completion of marathons, triathlons, and even Ironmans (Iron*women*, to be more exact). Through their training regiments, there was a natural process of stepping into stretch: building endurance and increasing capacity in the athlete's mind and body. Eventually, they accomplished something that may not have been possible before.

When Jacqueline's marathon day finally came, she hadn't ever run the entire 26.2 miles. It was another physical (and mental) stretch. Over time, she had changed her body's capacity for distance and her mental strength to persevere. Around mile twenty-two, her knees were starting to hurt. She was beyond tired. Her whole body felt like it was about to give out. She wasn't sure she could make it. But having trained, she knew her body's limits.

The final stretch of that first marathon run was seared in her brain and body. She recalls the memories as if they happened yesterday. She focused on her breathing and checked her Garmin. Three miles left. She could do this. She had run three miles so many times before. Before she knew it, she only had one mile left. She heard cheering in front of her and thought she heard her name. She looked up to see her boyfriend had joined her for the last mile. She fought back tears and shook off her exhaustion as they ran the last mile together.

Wrapped in a foil blanket, she collapsed on the ground. Her heart was beating so hard it felt like it was about to burst. She had done something she wasn't sure she could do. Pushing past the edge of her former comfort zone had stretched her ability to imagine what she could accomplish. As her family and friends celebrated with her, someone jokingly asked when she would be signing up for another race. She laughed. Years later, she's run marathons in multiple cities and continues to push herself to her further limits. One mile at a time, she found a space where she could routinely break her barriers.

Jacqueline's story is one of stretch. Ultimately, stepping into stretch enabled her to achieve a goal. Stretch changed her mind and body, allowing her to achieve something incredible. Her story is also an example of the Comfort, Stretch, Panic model in action. These three states function as a continuum rather than steps. The boundaries aren't always clear or distinct. At first, our capacity for stretch might be pretty limited. Our ability to stretch might start as incredibly narrow, or we might panic very quickly. But over time and with practice, we become adept at feeling into the edges of our comfort zone. Our stretch capacity grows.

Think about dipping your toes into the ocean. Even on a warm day in the early summer, water temperatures off the mid-Atlantic coast may only be in the sixties. At first, the cool water may be a shock to the system. A wave that splashes onto your legs might make you catch your breath. But continuing to wade into the water allows the system to assimilate. Before long, the cool, lapping water becomes a welcome sensation.

Our individual capacity for stretch is unique, so what works for one person may not work for another. Here are a few ways to support stepping into stretch:

1. **Establish a baseline:** Become aware of where your comfort, stretch, and panic zones live. Determine what they feel like, explore their size, and where their edges exist. Map out the current boundaries of your comfort and stretch zones. Knowing where we begin allows us to make more precise choices, stepping into stretch more seamlessly.

2. **Embrace fluidity:** Moving toward stretch isn't a one-way street. In marathon training, the distances don't increase incrementally until you reach the end goal. There is give and take, back and forth. Moments of more considerable stretch, combined with rest and rejuvenation, enable a steady and sustainable increase in our overall ability.

3. **Self-care and compassion:** The goal is stretch, not injury or harm. Too much pressure and stress can cause damage, and not just to our nervous system. Rather than trying to "get there" all at once, break down the process into more manageable steps into stretch. Start with aiming for "just one more" each day. Soon, the stretch capacity will have grown beyond what was previously possible.

Initially, we may be caught off guard by situations that stretch us. Eventually, we recognize stretch isn't reactive; it's responsive. Stepping further into stretch offers opportunities to seek out discomfort. This tactic helps us grow, shift, and change. In an interview with CNN, Marissa Mayer, information technology executive, cofounder of Sunshine Contacts, and former president and CEO of Yahoo!, reflects: "I always did something I was a little not ready to do. I think that's how you grow. When there's that moment of 'Wow, I'm not really sure I can do this,' and you push through those moments, that's when you have a breakthrough" (Taylor 2012).

I love stories of strong women. Stories of women in leadership positions who make bold contributions to the way we approach our lives and sometimes provocatively ask us to move outside ourselves. They push us to think bigger, bolder, and in ways that stretch us. Observing my own experiences and those of so many people in my life, I realized how easy it was to stay solidly in a comfort zone. It becomes easy to live on autopilot and not ask questions, think bigger, or dig deeper.

Determining why it was so hard to move toward things that make us uncomfortable seemed crucial. It's as important to understand what can help us move beyond our edges as knowing where they are. As I got curious about this topic, I came across the work of Farrah Storr. As the author of *The Discomfort Zone: How to Get What You Want by Living Fearlessly*, she has extensively researched this topic. Storr describes a phenomenon she calls brief moments of discomfort, or "BMDs." BMDs are "transitory moments of tension as you stand in the doorway of transformation" (Storr 2018, 2:44).

Storr is an accomplished journalist and former editor-in-chief for the UK editions of *Elle* and *Cosmopolitan*. In her TEDx Talk titled "The Discomfort Zone," she shares how she threw herself into "her first genuine moment of discomfort" at the age of twenty. Having grown up with siblings who shielded her from most of the challenges of adolescence, she made choices that mirrored theirs—mainly because it's what they did and seemed like a "right" next step. But she realized she was living a relatively static life. Wanting to find who she was and who she had the potential to become, she booked a one-way ticket to Paris at the age of twenty-one.

On the surface, that might not seem like an uncomfortable choice. For some, it might even sound glamorous. But it was quite a stretch for a young woman who had never lived with anyone other than her family, never traveled alone, and didn't speak French. She was deeply uncomfortable and well within her discomfort zone. But she realized the experiences as a whole weren't that painful. They were actually just BMDs. She realized, "as I dealt with each one of them, I started to notice small transformations taking place within me" (Storr 2018, 8:43).

I have encountered this same type of situation before, where brief moments of discomfort resulted in transformational changes. I had a friend in college who had never been outside of her small town before beginning undergrad. Our university home was nestled in the middle of the Central Illinois cornfields. Although it wasn't geographically far from the farm where she grew up, it seemed a world away. We met in one of our first classes, and her wide, darting eyes made it evident she was less than comfortable in this new and sprawling environment.

I noticed she was packing her bag very slowly once the class ended. I gently asked if she knew how to get to wherever she was going next. Looking down, she sheepishly admitted she wasn't quite sure. I told her I was new, too, and offered that we could walk together if she wanted some company. Although she didn't say much on our way across the quad, she finally let a smile peek out. Over time, timid smiles grew into bounding laughter. We walked across the quad together every Friday after class for the rest of the semester.

About a year later, I was waiting in line at a coffee shop when I heard a familiar laugh behind me. She ran over to give me a big hug. I was shocked at how different she seemed. A wide, open, and infectious smile was the backdrop for her words. Her hand rested on my shoulder as she spoke. "You know, I have to thank you. When we met, just the thought of saying hello to someone new made me so uncomfortable. I didn't think I could do it. But you showed me the only *really* hard part is the first hello. Now, I try to say hello to at least one new person a day. I've made so many friends since last year! And I don't even remember the 'old' me that was too scared even to try."

My friend's experience is another type of stretch. Personal stretch has a different flavor than stretching our physical limits, willpower, or capacity. Sometimes intentionally moving toward discomfort can help us grow. In their research on the relationship between discomfort and motivation, Kaitlin Woolley and Ayelet Fishbach discovered actively seeking the inherent discomfort in growth can be motivating, and embracing discomfort as a sign of progress rather than avoiding it is recommended (2022). Their experiments included taking improvisation classes to increase self-confidence, working through difficult emotions by journal writing, and engaging in conversation with those having opposing political views. An essential part of their research included the role of "reappraising" the discomfort—redefining discomfort's purpose from simply being something uncomfortable to a skill that supports and encourages change.

Growth is a series of daily decisions. We make choices to either move back toward what is safe and comfortable or forward toward growth. Discomfort—stretch—is a key to change, growth, and transformation. Rather than stretch being a painful struggle, perhaps we can think of it as a challenge that can strengthen us. Or as public figure Lewis Howes believes, "Greatness is living life outside of your comfort zone" (Howes 2016).

Looking at the reach and impact Lewis Howes has created, it might be easy to forget that achieving change doesn't happen overnight. With multiple books, a wildly successful podcast, and a brand that offers resources for achieving personal, interpersonal, and business greatness, Howes has devoted his life to empowerment. A former athlete who sustained a career-ending injury early on, he found himself living on his sister's couch. He was unsure where, why, or how he would move forward.

He started reaching out to those he admired. Curious about their stories and pathways to success, he began learning. Throughout all he has achieved, fear and discomfort were always an earmark of how to move forward. Although he now regularly speaks on stage in crowd-filled arenas, public speaking initially terrified him. Instead of shying away from it, however, he relentlessly stretched himself. He sought regular opportunities to engage and mentors to get feedback from, and ultimately meet with success. Having learned to lean into the initial discomfort of this skill, it still isn't something he takes for granted. "Speaking is no different than staying in shape; it's not something you get, it's something you maintain" (Howes 2012).

Maintaining stretch isn't always easy, but developed as a new habit, it becomes a way of continuously exploring, navigating, and remaining open to change. Helen's story is an excellent example of what stretching as an ongoing choice looks like in action. I wasn't expecting a call, so when my phone started ringing one Saturday afternoon, it startled me. I didn't recognize the number I saw on the caller ID. Most often, I'd let these calls go to voicemail, but since I had a few minutes, I decided to pick up.

"Hello?"

"Hi, I'm looking for Lisa DeAngelis. And the Alexander Technique. Is this the right number?" Her mixture of excitement and urgency brought a smile to my face.

"You have the right number!" I said with a chuckle. "Whom do I have the pleasure of speaking with?"

"Oh, good. Well, I'm Helen, Lisa. And I'm ready to change. You can help me with that, right?"

I had never met someone quite like Helen. At eighty-one years old, she was a widow who had never had children, and had lived alone since her second husband died almost two decades earlier. She had found my website, read up on my work as a holistic change practitioner, and wanted to come to learn—to change. As we discussed the logistics of meeting, I was concerned it might be too much for her to manage. Coming to my home studio required her to take the Metra into the city, transfer train lines, and then tackle the stairs to my third-story walk-up.

I was surprised to hear her say, "It would be an adventure." And although it was a little nerve-wracking—it had been quite a while since she had to make a train connection—she was up for the challenge. To the third-floor walk-up, she responded she didn't get enough exercise anyways.

She was tall and stately and always well-dressed. She had mostly lost the use of her left arm due to a bout with shingles years before, but other than that, she managed to get herself around the world fairly easily, and always with a smile on her face. Some weeks she would show up for our work together with a little less energy or in some pain, and I'd ask her if she wanted to take it easy. She'd laugh as she'd say, "Well, thank you for asking. But what's the point in taking it easy when there's so much I still want to do? Maybe we just go a tad bit slower today."

Although they winded her, she insisted the stairs were essential since she couldn't exercise much anymore. We worked on expanding her range of motion so she could try tennis lessons. She would laugh about how she had "two left feet," but it didn't keep her from wanting to work on her balance. When she was younger, she had always wanted to be a dancer.

Most days, she wasn't sure how to get from here to there, but that was where our work came into the picture. I'd help her try something new physically. She'd feel a little uncomfortable at first, sometimes unsteady on her feet, but would remind herself if she didn't try something new, she'd never know whether she could.

As we continued to work together, I learned more about her story and her approach to life (and change). After her husband died, she made a promise to herself. She would say "yes" to everything she wanted to do. Traveling, taking up new hobbies, and trying new things became choices she actively made. Her sense of moving toward things she didn't yet know or understand exhibited the tools for change on display. Helen's choices were brave, resilient, and admirable. She reminded me that our ability to stretch is a conscious choice.

Whether on the baseball field or arriving at mile twenty-six, stretching can be strategically used to help achieve our physical goals. Moving toward discomfort creates opportunities to explore bigger and bolder paths in our personal lives. A mindset of stretching as a means to change establishes the habit of growth, no matter our age or stage of life. Stepping into stretch helps us surpass the limitations of how far we can go.

CHAPTER 7

Permission to Launch

My legs shook beneath me as the instructor caught the swinging bar and showed me where to place my hands. The platform was higher up than it had seemed from the ground. Even though the harness I wore wasn't exactly comfortable, I was more than grateful to have it on.

A few moments before, I had found myself tentatively climbing up a ladder, rung by rung. I wasn't sure who I was silently cursing more: my friend for talking me into joining her for an outdoor trapeze class or myself for agreeing to go. I watched a few graceful nine- and ten-year-olds launch themselves off the very same platform where I now stood, their bodies moving in gorgeous swinging arcs. It was their first time, too, but they looked like full-fledged trapeze artists, landing on the net with easy, buoyant bounces. I wasn't sure my experience would be the same.

On the ground far below, I could see my friend's excitement. Cheering in support, she offered an exuberant wave. I needed all the help I could get. Comforting reassurance from the instructor's calls at least gave me something to focus on. I was grateful he would help cue me. All I had to do was not overthink, he promised. As directed, I inched to the platform's edge and leaned my weight forward. A hot rush swept from the pit of my stomach all the way up to my head. Dizzy for a moment, I almost backed out. Time seemed to stop as I watched the rhythmic swinging of the cables below, lulling me forward.

How do I know when to jump? What am I even doing? I can't do this.

At that moment, I was waiting for permission to let go. But the choice was all mine.

Well. Here goes nothing. I closed my eyes, took a deep breath, and jumped.

Are you waiting for permission?

It's a question I've asked myself countless times over the years. I had come up against many intersections in my life where the potential of something new or different was just around the corner, or just up ahead. Yet, something kept me where I was—as if my feet were stuck in the mud. At times, I could see the summit ahead but seemed unable to move forward.

Awestruck, I would devour the stories of people who could fearlessly leap, giving themselves permission to take risks. Carving new pathways for their lives was bold and courageous. I remember the first time I read Elizabeth Gilbert's memoir *Eat, Pray, Love: One Woman's Search for Everything Across*

Italy, India, and Indonesia. She took me, and her millions of readers through the years, on a year-long search to discover who she was and what she wanted. She spent months relishing in Italy's lush culture and endless opportunities for pasta, seeking spiritual connection at an ashram in India, and searching for balance (and finding love) in Bali. It was an inspirational adventure: indulgent, brave, and raw.

I could never do that.

I wasn't struggling at the time, but I wasn't happy. I knew there was more to my life, but I wasn't sure which way to go. I wanted a change. Gilbert's words seemed to ring in my ears: "Happiness is the consequence of personal effort. You fight for it, strive for it, insist upon it, and sometimes even travel around the world looking for it. You have to participate relentlessly in the manifestations of your own blessings. And once you have achieved a state of happiness, you must never become lax about maintaining it. You must make a mighty effort to keep swimming upward into that happiness forever, to stay afloat on top of it" (Gilbert 2010, 260).

I've often gone back to that page of the book where I emphatically underlined Gilbert's text, scribbling "Yes!" in the margin of the page. Something about her story, and those words, helped give me permission to participate in building pathways along the road of my own personal and professional journeys toward happiness. My degree in music education and subsequent work as a full-time nanny weren't exactly stellar resume supports for a job in Commercial Real Estate, but I still applied. Years later, I wasn't sure how all the pieces would come together to enable me to move halfway across the country, amid a global pandemic, but I had given myself the permission to dream it into reality.

Reflecting on her memoir in a conversation with Oprah Winfrey, Gilbert shared, "I feel like, in a way, *Eat, Pray, Love* kind of was a permission slip from the principal's office that said you are allowed to ask yourself some really important questions about your life. You are allowed to take accountability and ownership for your own journey" (Gilliard et al. 2014).

This wasn't the first time I had heard this reference to permission slips. The analogy was a reminder that we each can allow the freedom of choice we so desperately yearn for. In *Braving the Wilderness*, Brené Brown spoke of giving herself license through this act of permission. Inspired by her children's school permission slips, she started physically writing herself permission slips. Sometimes it was to enjoy something. Other times it was to stop being afraid or to have fun. Though it only took a few moments, it was a powerful act. It represented something much bigger than simply words on a page. Brown reflects, "But as with the permission slips you give your kids, they may have permission to go to the zoo, but they still need to get on the bus. Set the intention. Follow through" (2017, 20). Permission as an intentional act becomes an unrelenting commitment to moving toward truth and, in doing so, offers us freedom of choice.

What does permission look like in choice and action? How can we embrace permission in a way that supports our ongoing growth? Sometimes, it starts with simple questions that can foster deep connections, not only with others but also within ourselves.

Hannah Austin is now the successful founder of SheShatters, LLC—a movement that helps women "burn bright so they don't burn out." The creation of her company meets a deep need to help professionals suffering from burnout. She works with women and organizations to find balance in a world that often pushes for productivity at the expense of health and wellness. But achieving her present-day success didn't happen overnight. Only a few years prior, she wouldn't have anticipated the way her story would unfold.

An MBA with twenty years of experience, she managed a large outpatient team for a Fortune 500 health care company. Her goal was CEO, and she poured herself into work. Juggling two cell phones, daily double-booked meetings, and a dizzying, relentless work pace for almost two decades meant that in many ways, she had become her job. It defined her and her purpose in life.

She never expected she would become a patient in one of the emergency rooms where she worked. Her habits and patterns led to fatigue and burnout. Her doctors were frank in sharing she was simply not well and needed to take care of herself. How would she even begin? What did moving on mean? What did she really want? In a sobering conversation with her husband, she recalls his important observation: "You've been done for a while. Why are you still holding on?"

She continued asking herself important, catalytic questions: "What am I holding on to? And why am I holding on so tight when I don't even want it?"

Hannah needed permission. Realizing she couldn't trust herself to go back to work in a way that preserved her health, she quit. She took three months off. Lost, anxious, and unsure of what to do, she sought out respite and healing with therapists, spiritual gurus, and life coaches. To get down to the core of who she was, she needed to excavate her old patterns and layers, step by step. That awareness created the necessity to change. She understood it was finally time to move on and pursue what actually brought her joy.

Building the next phase of her life and career required constructing her own ladder of permission, which allowed her vision and company to grow. She continued to give herself permission to explore new pathways and think bigger. Although it hasn't been without its setbacks and challenges, she has committed to a certain aliveness in her life and work. She has shown up with adaptability and resilience in moments when things were difficult and with courage when there weren't yet clients to fill her calendar. She reflects that often "we only see real life in black and white ways. If we even try to take little steps and we fumble, or we stop, or we fall, that setback is so much harder. It pulls us back to the dark."

In order to "hardwire" the pathway of permission on the road to change, it's necessary to eliminate the binary thinking that is so pervasive in our culture. It's easy to fall into the trap of thinking there is only one "right" way to move forward. It's tempting to believe that once we start climbing the ladder of permission, there's only one direction we can go. In reality, temporary setbacks or challenges don't have to throw us off course. They aren't permanent decisions, just useful opportunities to learn while establishing new baselines and goals for the next steps forward, and up, the ladder. Growth and emergence become a nonlinear climb.

Plenty of tools exist to help us understand ourselves better. The Enneagram is one of these tools, based on the concept of nine interrelated personality types. This personality identification system doesn't aim to limit or typecast our character traits and habits. Rather, it's designed to support us in gaining awareness of our fears and tendencies, so we can ultimately grow. It doesn't focus on defining who we are in a fixed or permanent way. The system is dynamic and accounts for the fact that people change constantly.

The Enneagram offers a continuous guide to self-observation. Like climbing the rungs of a ladder, it becomes a map we can use to chart where we are in our development at any given time. Even in moments that appear to be great leaps in moving forward, there are always incremental steps that move us toward our goals. We live then, not in a definition of who we are, but in a state of exploring how to live out our full potential.

This, too, is how the continuum of permission functions. Awareness and observation can be useful tools and help us to discover where we are in relation to where we want to be. Having more permission, or making bigger jumps in the process, isn't necessarily "better" or "worse." Climbing the ladder of permission simply asks us to determine what levels of permission are required. We can explore this topic through a few important questions:

- Are we aware permission is needed?
- Is permission being sought internally or externally?
- Do we have permission to dream bigger and aspire for something different?
- What is required to climb another rung of the ladder?

In Hannah's case, her job was a way of life. Permission was an important factor as she began approaching her story differently. Her husband's encouragement offered her the support to make important choices. Expanded permission to choose her health and well-being allowed her the space to grow and stretch herself. Still setting goals to achieve her dreams, Hannah's capacity to give, and take, permission has launched more than just her ability to make different choices. Today, she has a thriving business, community, and podcast, and her work continues to help women on their journey from burnout to finding their joy. Hannah's book, *Hello Head, Meet Heart*, shares how women can tap into themselves in order to live their most extraordinary lives.

It's crucial to recognize there is an important baseline for permission: safety. In their research on psychological safety, Amy C. Edmondson and Zhike Lei conclude that "the interpersonal experience of psychological safety is argued to be foundational for enabling behaviors essential to learning and change" (2014). Research on psychological safety, as well as polyvagal theory, has proven that, although everything you want may be on the other side of fear, establishing safety is crucial to the ability to move toward change.

In his book, *The Pocket Guide to the Polyvagal Theory: The Transformative Power of Feeling Safe*, Dr. Stephen Porges states, "Outside the realm of conscious awareness, our nervous system is continuously evaluating risk in the environment, making judgments, and setting priorities for behaviors that are adaptive. These processes occur without our awareness and without the conscious mental processes that we attribute to the 'executive' functions involved in decision-making"

(Porges 2017, 55). Taking risks may not only be something that stretches us outside our comfort zone but also a very basic function of our evolutionary safety.

This safety is much more fundamental to our adaptive body system than simply employing positive thinking or changing our thought patterns. In some cases, including those of trauma, a mismatch in our system occurs, causing it to perceive a lack of safety. This results in a state of fight, flight, or freeze that prevents our social engagement system from coming fully online (Porges 2009). As a first step, it can be important to determine what feelings are showing up when resistance to change—or permission—arise. Fear and risk are not without discomfort, but with strong scaffolding in place, we can once again begin to climb the ladder of permission.

For Meridith Grundei, exploring this idea led her to create a podcast with cohost Joseph Bennett titled *Are You Waiting for Permission?* She resonated with the concept as a creative person, as well as a human living in the real world, reflecting that there were many decisions she had made where she didn't wait for permission. It also illuminates a larger question around permission and what happens when the systems of our culture don't always offer us the permission we seek. She attests, "The truth is there's never going to be the right amount of money. There's never going to be the right amount of time. It ends up being a journey of how you want to live your life in the moment." Her goal is to help people feel empowered to take risks so they can ultimately live the lives they want.

Stories of success, permission, and choice inspire us. But at times, it seems there is an insurmountable gap between where we are and where we want to go. It can be hard to ignore the fear we feel when the change we want to make doesn't feel close. Meridith reflects on this challenge, drawing on her background in theater and improvisation. In improv, it can appear what happens on stage is all spur of the moment and the creativity and genius of its execution is a seamless reaction to whatever arises. Although part of the art of improvisation is just that, it's not the whole story. There is some "making stuff up on the spot," but there is also still a structure that's utilized. Meridith advises, "You still need to develop a container, whatever that road map looks like for you, so that you know exactly the steps you're going to take to get from A to B."

In Meridith's personal life, she and her family knew they wanted change and needed to figure out what the "more" for their lives looked like. They listed and eventually rented their house on Airbnb. Despite slim financial margins, they decided to spend a year traveling by RV. They "road-schooled" their first-grade daughter, flying back when their work required. An unexpected breakdown in Memphis forced them to reflect on whether Tennessee could be a long-term landing place for their family. When they started running out of money, they ventured down to Central Mexico. It was a place where they could maximize their resources while taking in as much culture and experience as possible. It offered them an unforgettable adventure. Ultimately, they found a new home, and the best place for their family, in New York City. It wasn't a place they ever thought they'd be. But working to climb their ladder of permission ultimately allowed them freedom of choice in embracing change, and a life, they built.

The parts of our stories that lead us to whatever is "next" on our change journey are unfinished endings each of us must write. Inspiration from the successful experiences of others can stir something deep inside us, but we are the only ones who can climb our own ladder of permission. This concept was initially a challenge for me. In fact, it was one of the reasons I desperately searched for someone who would grant me permission to change. Repeatedly, I was only left with more questions. The answers didn't—couldn't—come from the outside. No one could write my story for me.

Although I wasn't always sure I trusted, or even liked, the "me" I saw in the mirror, slowly, I began to recognize I needed her. Not only did I need her, but I also humbly understood I had to make friends with her, rather than avoiding, shaming, or judging her. That messy, imperfect, and often scared version of myself was the *only* one who could take me closer to where I wanted to be. She was the only one who could lead me to the next chapter of my journey. I realized if I stopped long enough to notice, she had already let go of my hand. She was waving me on from the ground below as I gave myself permission to make my next vision a reality.

What had I been waiting for?

Choice lived in the space—the gap—between where I was and where I wanted to be. Instead of feeling like the path was insurmountable, I discovered I could construct a ladder to help me get there. Walking toward that first rung, I could give myself permission to start climbing. As James Clear shares in *Atomic Habits*, "Many situations in life are similar to going on a hike: the view changes once you start walking.

You don't need all the answers right now. New paths will reveal themselves if you have the courage to get started" (Clear 2022).

When our desire to see what's "up there" is greater than the risk of staying on the ground, we learn where and when to start. Giving ourselves permission allows us freedom. We make choices. When we try new things, we learn. Sometimes when we take risks we stumble or fall. Each step helps strengthen our capacity to be in stretch, reminding us the view changes as we climb the ladder.

High on that trapeze platform was one of the countless moments in my life where I had to make a choice. Looking back, each time I gave myself permission to climb another rung of the ladder, my pathway became clearer. Should I listen to my gut or an expert who told me I needed reconstructive jaw surgery at eighteen years old? Even if I wasn't qualified on paper, should I go for that new job? I recognized that even if a move wasn't the right choice, and I ended up moving again in a few years, I had done it. I knew I wasn't ever going to be a trapeze artist, but I would still try it.

By the end of that summer day, I had not only been successful on the trapeze in multiple runs, but I had also completed a moving catch. Exhilarated, my heart beat hard and strong as I released my hands and bounced onto the net below. I remember thinking how free it felt to fly, even if just for a few moments. I understood that in order to launch myself forward into the life I truly wanted to lead, permission was an essential step: to start, to climb, and to soar.

CHAPTER 8

A View from Above

An unprecedented first took place on a hot July Sunday in 1969. The live feed was a feat of engineering, and in a moment of collective awe, an estimated 650 million people watched as Neil Armstrong took "one small step for a man, one giant leap for mankind" (Killingsworth 2019). Incredible technological advances enabled this historic event to occur. Beyond just the "space race," these developments affected industries far beyond. Polymer fabric and breathing masks used to navigate the moon's conditions are still used in fire departments, emergency response services, and other military and industrial applications. The total impact of this event was not just limited to these iconic moments and valuable innovations; it was also responsible for important shifts in perspective.

Current technology allows us to search, find, and view pictures of our solar system with a single click of a button. However, the real experience is still limited to those who have had the opportunity to travel to space. Initially, space exploration focused on discovering what's "out there," but catching a glimpse of our planet from outer space proved to be a permanently altering experience for astronauts. Frank White coined "The Overview Effect" in 1987 to describe this "profound reaction to viewing the Earth outside its atmosphere" (White 1987).

Astronauts' life-changing stories of seeing Earth from this shifted perspective have been documented in the short film *Overview* by Planetary Collective. In this documentary, philosopher David Loy reflects on this phenomenon: "It was quite a shock; I don't think any of us had any expectations about how it would give us such a different perspective. I think the focus had been: 'We're going to the stars; we're going to other planets.' And suddenly we look back at ourselves, and it seems to imply a new kind of self-awareness" (Reid 2012, 1:13).

A shift in perspective doesn't just change us in a moment; it can change how we see things permanently. Like turning the wheel of a kaleidoscope, shapes and colors shift and merge to create new and endless patterns right before our eyes. When we go back to look again, it's different—changed. New and fresh, it offers us another glimpse into what is possible when we keep looking.

Definitions of "perspective" found in *Merriam-Webster.com Dictionary* (2023) include *"the interrelation in which a subject or its parts are mentally viewed"* and *"the capacity to view things in their true relations or relative importance."* Much like the lens of a camera, this interrelation allows us to employ a familiar camera technique: zooming in and out. As we learn to shift this lens of perspective, so does our relationship to exploring opportunities ahead of us.

My brother is an aerospace optometrist in the United States Navy and has been an avid photographer for many years. I was always impressed by his ability to delve into, study, and learn new skills, but this one was especially impressive. Years into watching his work develop, my favorite observation was the difference between what I saw in any given moment with my two eyes and what he captured through the lens of his camera. I'd always think we were looking at the same thing, but when I saw his pictures—the final product—they often revealed a perspective I had never considered.

Two photographers taking a picture of the same subject with the same camera could result in two drastically different outcomes based on how they see and capture the image. Different lenses can create altered perspectives. Factor in the application of their skill and interpretation of the subject, and the options become endless. This is the power of a perspective shift. As photographer Rick Smolan reflected: "What amazes me is that you can have ten different photographers in the same room and you see ten different rooms. You realize how much of it is the person's perspective, rather than the situation itself" (Cruz 2012).

What was most fascinating in my brother's case was how his lens choice allowed him to capture an image in a unique and particular way, often a way I'm not sure I would have ever thought of. Occasionally, he would zoom in on something I hadn't even noticed, pulling in focus so tightly the rest of the image seemed to fall away. I'd see the picture later and marvel at how a shift of perspective created an entirely new visual experience. Zooming out would create a spectacular scene, giving me the impression I was seeing a familiar landscape for the first time. In the case of a particular lens like the fish-eye, the image would be intentionally distorted, so the viewer was asked to consider the subject in a unique way. By orienting the view in a completely different manner, the final product resulted in an entirely shifted space. As we hone in on and navigate the change process, we can become aware of how to optimize our view and how this lens of perspective can be utilized to find, create, or expand opportunities.

From age five, Erika Knierim knew she wanted to become a lawyer. Perhaps she had caught wind of the profession from a scene in a movie or on TV. No one in her family was an attorney, and she didn't even know anyone who was. Whatever the inspiration, she never wavered. In college, her dad suggested she diversify her classes but she wasn't interested. To her admission, her confidence and focus in her early chosen profession were baffling, perhaps, but always steady.

She went on to narrow her focus and specialize her studies. Eventually, she became a successful public defender. She advocated the best she could for her clients in an inherently flawed system. The work was intense, and often violent. As the years wore on, she found it harder and harder to maintain a sense of balance. Difficulties in the workplace made it clear staying wasn't healthy or sustainable.

Erika became aware something needed to change. She started therapy. Expanding her social circles, she invested time in things she enjoyed outside work: philanthropy, music, and art. She kept trying to approach challenges from a process perspective, knowing there had to be a solution to the problem she could find. A new job was a necessity—maybe even a new career. But it seemed hard to find the right path or see any other opportunities. Her narrow focus had left her untrained for little else.

Through a series of conversations, she got an unexpected opportunity: a meeting with one of the principals at a prominent Chicago investment firm. She showed up dressed in a sharp navy suit and a simple string of pearls, her dark hair tied back in a low, sleek ponytail. She planned to pitch an idea for a cultural partnership event to see if there could be a connection. Although she met with success that day, the result wasn't what she expected. She was stopped in the middle of her conversation and asked to quit her job and come work for the firm.

Her initial response was a laugh. "I don't even know what you do. I barely know the difference between a stock and a bond."

"You're smart. You'll figure it out."

"You've lost your mind."

She left the meeting and called her brother. Pressingly, he urged, "Erika, this is it. It's not what you thought it would be, but you don't know what other options are available, and these jobs do not fall into people's laps. They just don't."

Recalling her state of nervousness and fear, she remembers uttering the words, "But, Tonio. What if I fail?"

"What is failure? Failure doesn't exist. Not unless you let it exist in your life."

It was one of the most important conversations she would ever have, and something clicked for her at that moment. She had been on autopilot for a long time, thinking her "work" had been done. At some level, she thought she had achieved what she set out to accomplish in life, and that was all there was. Her perspective on her career, opportunity, and even failure had become so zoomed in she risked passing up this unexpected opportunity. She found herself unsure and without a clear view of what was ahead. Adapted from the words of Les Brown, she couldn't see the picture while she was in the frame.

What is the next step when it is hard to see what's ahead? How do we shift perspective and alter our view? Leveraging this lens of perspective begins with a shift of mindset.

In her book *Mindset*, Stanford University psychologist Carol Dweck looks at the difference between fixed and growth mindsets. A growth mindset is focused on improvement and the belief that things, and you, are malleable and can constantly change. On the other hand, a fixed mindset is static and often focused on judgment. Whether applied to learning, math scores, child development, or athletics, Dweck feels a mindset change is much more than just changing your mind. She believes, "Mindset change is not about picking up a few pointers here and there. It's about seeing things in a new way. When people [...] change to a growth mindset, they change from a judge-and-be-judged framework to a learn-and-help-learn framework. Their commitment is to growth, and growth takes plenty of time, effort, and mutual support" (2007, 254).

Combining a growth mindset and shifting the lens of perspective to create opportunities requires zooming in and out.

By determining the level of focus (zoom) we have been seeing through, we can intentionally choose to shift to another, and see what we can notice then. Stephen Covey, author of *The 7 Habits of Highly Effective People*, reinforces this idea: "We must look at the lens through which we see the world, as well as the world we see, and that the lens itself shapes how we interpret the world" (2013, 25).

Any situation is ultimately about the view from which we see it. As we learn to establish, and reestablish where we are, we can choose when and where to adjust and focus our lens. Zooming in and out becomes an invaluable skill to hone for shifting our perspective. In doing so, we see what we can see from another view. If we are too zoomed in, we may not be able to see another opportunity. Too zoomed out, it may be hard to focus on a concrete next step.

Ultimately, utilizing this skill of fluidly zooming in and zooming out creates a loop of growth and opportunity, helping prevent us from remaining static for too long. Because this cyclical process also creates feedback, it becomes more difficult to dwell on mistakes. We can continuously lean on the tool "ARC"—change tools of adaptability, resilience, and courage—to help counteract setbacks and allow us to continue expanding our construction zone of change rather than getting stuck in stages of the process.

I love how Barney Saltzberg utilizes this concept in his book *Beautiful Oops!*, where seeming mistakes, setbacks, or "failures" are turned into inspired opportunities for creativity. A paper tear becomes the mouth of an alligator. An errant drip of paint becomes the wheels of a car. A coffee cup stain becomes the perfect landing pad for a frog. As the back of the book proudly states: "When you think you have made a mistake (and what kid or grown-up hasn't), think of it as an opportunity to make something beautiful" (Saltzberg 2010). Whether beautiful, new, or unexpected, shifting our perspective can offer us an entirely new experience.

The term "30,000-foot view" is often used in business to describe a broad overview approach from a height where the big picture can be more easily observed. Sometimes big ideas show up when you least expect them. There are also moments in life that require intense zooming in. In these cases, using a magnifying glass to dig into something small but crucial can clear the pathway for the next stage of the journey.

I invite you to play with this idea. It's important to figure out how far the shift of our own lens can go:

- Sometimes the process starts with zooming out to catch the view from across the street. When we're too zoomed in, and our focus is fixed, it can be hard to take such a giant leap so suddenly. And that's okay. Take a walk across the street, check it out, and then come back inside if needed. Maybe tomorrow you can try something new.

- A balcony view takes things a little further. What happens when our vantage point is now from above? Everything can still be seen with pretty clear detail, but sometimes what went unnoticed out on the horizon becomes a new and unexpected destination to explore.

- What happens if you zoom out to thirty-thousand feet? Perhaps there are things you hadn't noticed before. Seemingly divergent points in your life may find patterns of convergence when approached from a big-picture perspective. This is also the space to generate big ideas and think out of the figurative, or literal, box.

- Zoom in again to see what you notice. Try doing this quickly at first. The next time, see how slowly the descent can be made. What are you drawn to zoom in on? What happens when something leaves your field of vision? Where do you ultimately land?

Erika's utilization of the lens of perspective helped her see opportunities. It also didn't stop when she decided to take the job with the financial firm; it was just the next step. The way the role's compensation was structured, she had three years to build up a book of business, and a lot to learn, before working solely on commission. She rolled up her sleeves and got to work. She passed her Series 7 and Series 66 exams, two important industry qualification and certification tests. But just over a year later, the world shut down due to the COVID-19 pandemic, and everything shifted again.

Being unsure of what opportunities lay ahead is a difficult situation, and it would have been easy for Erika to get stuck in a fixed, limited mindset. But she leaned heavily on the process of zooming in and out. Using this tool and applying a growth mindset over the next turbulent months, she took steps to shift her perspective and continued exploring and creating opportunities:

She joined an experimental social audio platform called Clubhouse and started listening intently. Seeing where the new edges of industries were going, she tuned in to the fresh and relevant conversations people were having, taking in everything she could. (Zoom out.)

She found a new and enticing area of interest—cryptocurrency and the world of NFTs. She read over 110 books on the cutting-edge subject, giving herself a crash course in a new industry. (Zoom in.)

Unsure where it might eventually take her, she started her own consulting company. Working on referrals and making connections, she applied her informed perspective and solid legal background to a new professional arena, developing a completely unique offering. (Zoom out.)

Realizing her work in law was completely different from her new area of focus, she honed her interview skills and rewrote her resume to increase her relevance in a specialized field. (Zoom in.)

She would never have fathomed the opportunities that presented themselves. "There's a feeling of freedom that comes from recognizing you can live your life intentionally; when you take life on a day-to-day basis. You get to enjoy more of it, because you're not hanging on for dear life, just hoping that the right thing is going to pan out." Eventually, she landed a position with a global fintech company where she could apply her many skills in a new, forward-thinking space. But that too was short-lived. She was let go from her job a few months later after the company declared bankruptcy. Fully zooming out again, she saw that even though another door had closed, she caught a glimpse of a wide-open window.

The pathway had been paved, and Erika stepped into her next career move. She now embraces the title of founder and principal in her own company, Nomic Consulting. She cites her ability to intentionally shift her perspective as one of the main reasons she continues to grow, reaching unexpected destinations. "I don't really see decisions as good or bad anymore. I see them as opportunities. All the emotional work I've done has prepared me to step into this space—believing that I can be that woman. I can be the head of a company that is legitimate, has value, and that the work that needs to be done in that space is work that I, Erika Knierim, can do."

Shifting our perspective is about more than making a change. It's about learning how to navigate a continuum of views. Removing judgment, we recognize how we see something in any given moment is simply a product of our perspective.

I've looked at the world from thirty thousand feet more than a few times—not just figuratively. Inevitably, as my plane descends through the clouds, the view outside my window shifts. Blue sky, sun, and fluffy white clouds give way to a darker landscape, and I'm reminded what happens above and below can be drastically different. The weather reflects my rapidly changing perspective, and the entire mood shifts once we coast below the clouds. I note the traces of water tracking along the plane window's surface; it's raining.

Ten thousand feet isn't always the most comfortable place to be, especially for someone who grew up with severe motion sickness. Caught in the in-between, I want nothing more than to be back up in the clouds or down safely on land. As we inch closer to the ground, I pause, seeing the entire city appear through the view out my tiny window. It doesn't feel this small when I navigate the streets in real time. But from here, it reminds me of the Legos and Hot Wheels my little brother used to play with.

I'm reminded of all the places I want to go and the things I want to do. Instantly, I find myself thinking of the various ways I could make them all happen, seizing opportunity. The now nonexistent raindrops are slowly being replaced by a few glowing slivers of sunlight. We gently coast onto the runway with a few gentle bounces. Once again, the skyline off on the horizon looks more like I remembered—full of potential, excitement, and endless opportunity ahead.

CHAPTER 9

The Change Cycle

I let out a long exhale as I stepped back to admire my handiwork. After rummaging around the back of my closet, I found some balloons and a pendant banner from a baby shower I threw for a friend a year earlier. I spent the next hour carefully attaching decorations to otherwise bare walls in an all-too-quiet room. A few days before my thirty-sixth birthday, I desperately needed something to cheer me up. It had worked. It was the first thing that had made me smile in weeks. Just two weeks prior, Chicago had been put under a mandatory "stay at home" order; the SARS-COVID-19 virus was rampant across the US, and states quickly followed suit, locking down one by one.

I looked down at my watch and realized it was April 1st. Some April Fool's joke.

That birthday, technological greetings were the closest I came to sharing celebrations. Living alone meant isolation defined my new normal. Instead of a rousing party, I sat alone, watching as the sun streamed in through the window. The small bundle of balloons filling the otherwise empty corner of the room brought a smile to my face. Reflecting the light, the glitter on the pendant banner danced. Although it was a little gesture, the soft pink decorations that now adorned my walls reminded me there was something to find worth celebrating even in the most difficult of times.

In early 2020, COVID affected the entire world in a way no one could have imagined. It would be easy to say the events that followed simply changed us. Of course, they did. Our environment was changed too. And each of us also made changes as we responded to the world around us. Our next steps became a result of the choices we made—directly or indirectly—due to our unexpected, and shifted, circumstances.

In their research on nonlinear change, Adele M. Hayes et al. argue that destabilization can be a catalyst for personal change. "Ilya Prigogine, a Nobel laureate known for his theory of dissipative structures in chemistry, argues that instabilities play an important role in transformation and that 'most of reality, instead of being orderly, stable, and equilibrial, is seething and bubbling with change, disorder, and process' (Prigogine & Stengers, 1984, xv)" (Hayes et al. 2007). Destabilization can cause a loosening of old patterns and the opportunity for whole system reorganization. This can look like a shift in priorities, goals, motivations, and relationships or a deepening of inner strength, purpose, and spiritual connection.

Initially, I thought change needed a hero and there was a change code to be cracked. Perhaps finding an answer to the "what" would allow me to create a map to address the "how." I attempted to distill everything I learned about change into a formula, a framework, or a zone. If only the secret to change could be wrapped up with a pretty bow and presented as the perfect solution.

Perhaps change was like a recipe. If so, it would be essential to look at the ingredients, how much of each is needed, and when. Perhaps the magic was in the way it's all brought together:

> *Combine equal parts stretch, permission, and perspective.*
>
> *Gently fold in awareness, add a dash of nonjudgment, and mix it all together.*
>
> *For best results, pour into a pan coated with ARC— adaptability, resilience, and courage.*
>
> *Bake until fully risen and change reaches desired doneness.*
>
> *Let rest. Add a dollop of your inner knowing for sweetness, and garnish generously with any leftover courage.*
>
> *Serve and enjoy!*

But that felt limiting and reductionistic. It wasn't as simple as getting handed a formula or prescription. How much stretch do I need? When will it be done? How in the world do I fold in awareness? The answers wouldn't be found on a map with specific directions. Starting "here" and ending up somewhere in "the field of change" didn't seem to account for the process's intricacies, individuality, and personal nature. And where was "here," anyway?

Change is dynamic. It's the result of each of the choices we make and how they come to life. I have come to realize that rather than a prescription or step-by-step directions, change actually needs a new set of guiding principles and core values. This allows us to address, and embrace, change now and in an ongoing way. The beauty of change is in its potential, but the power of change is in choice.

There are over eight billion people worldwide, and no two people's change journeys are the same. But there are a few universal truths about change I've distilled:

- **Change is hard.** No matter how you sugarcoat it, growth is a painful process. Once we have compassion and acceptance for this truth, we can begin to learn how to make the process more natural and enjoyable.

- **Change is rarely linear.** As much as we can try to oversimplify the process, the path zigzags, winds, and jogs back and forth much more than it stays straight and narrow.

- **Change needs more of the things we might not expect.** Stepping back and observing rather than digging in and doing more work can help us see where we want to go. Ultimately, rather than a defined set of things to "do," it's about determining what will work for whom.

- **Change isn't something outside of us.** It's something we are in relationship with. In many ways, it's the ultimate creative process.

The creative process works in a cycle—gathering materials and information, working through an idea, and then, perhaps vitally, stepping away to allow space before coming back to integrate and generate a result. Change acts similarly. As I have reflected on and collected these many stories of change, there was a thread—a through line—in many of these approaches that cultivated the conditions for moving toward change actively and intentionally. Still, at the time I wasn't quite sure what. I now recognize different versions of what I have repeatedly seen and experienced. Always present was a cycle of continuously tapping into the process of change in a way that protects a vision while enabling exploration and action. Change looks much less like a straight line and more like the curving, winding pathways of the creative process.

Visual artist Kelly Kruse speaks about her artistic process and change with grace and clarity. As an artist, she translates a vision for a painting rather than aiming to replicate an idea she has in her head. Her visual devotional practice originally developed as a response to a battle with depression. Now, through her creative process she wrestles with beauty, history, and theology. Making nonrepresentational art allows her to engage with the wonder of the materials themselves. She discovers the limits of their application as she explores the way they take up space on a particular surface. Her process allows her to draw connections and translate meaning from material, texture, and color.

There are inevitable times when her process—a painting, for example—takes a different direction than she anticipated. Occasionally this results in a surprise—sometimes, color blends unexpectedly, or material acts differently than she would have thought. Especially when unanticipated, these surprises can spur a change in creative direction. Kruse is aware of the tendency of new artists to hate how their work is developing mid-process because it may not always line up with what they imagined in their heads. But she knows that as an artist, she has a choice.

Sometimes following the unexpected direction is the better choice. Other times, the vision of a piece needs to be reined in. Ultimately, it's about observing without judgment and then making a choice. Creating art is simply a dance of following and leading until the piece finds its way to life. Showing up in her professional world, she believes that to be an important truth of the creative process. At the end of our conversation, she reflected on how her art often echoes life's change process: "I accept the vision that I get like the spark instead of the thing that I must reproduce. I have to hold the whole process with a slightly open hand—because there are a lot of things I'm just not in control of."

As important as identifying our relationship to change is the need to learn how to use it and what it means. Beyond gathering the right tools and creating the conditions that make it possible to change, we must broaden our horizons and deepen our skills. As we step into the process, we discover and embrace The Change Cycle. The tools themselves are static. What makes them catalysts for growth and change is how we use, regulate, and leverage them:

- A bicycle is only useful as a mode of transportation when we get on and begin to pedal.
- Give two children a set of Tinkertoys, and they will build entirely different masterworks using the same pieces.
- Paint, brushes, and canvas only come to life when enlivened by the artist as tools to create.

The Change Cycle has emerged as a frame of reference for navigating change. Rather than a formula, like change, it's a process. It forms a set of guiding principles that allow change to come to life—not because of what we are doing, but because of how we are allowing it.

AWARENESS

In any period of change, there is a "before" and an "after." Awareness is the key to establishing a baseline. We start by asking ourselves the question: What don't I know? This determines our starting point. It's the phase of the cycle that's ripe for growth. We give ourselves permission to launch and make the choice to begin.

DIRECTION

Direction is the most active apex of the cycle, in which we choose what tools to leverage and what support will optimize our journey:

Do we need to stretch further?

Where do we need to give, or take, permission?

Can we shift our perspective?

Where do we need to lean into our ARC—adaptability, resilience, and courage—to support us?

What barriers up ahead can be avoided, worked around, or even dissolved?

We generate, move, and shift. We step into stretch. As the action happens and pieces are put together, movement begins.

NONJUDGMENTAL OBSERVATION
This is an essential part of The Change Cycle. It requires surrender and vulnerability. Taking on the role of an observer asks us to let go of judgment. Utilizing the lens of perspective—zooming in and out—allows us to see through unbiased eyes. In doing so, we can make choices that support us rather than getting stuck in our habits, barriers, or blind spots.

"RE"CYCLE
The "re" phase of any cycle is often bypassed. Reorient. Reflect. Reassess. Rest. Renew.

In our culture of productivity, it can be easy to forget this step is crucial to action. Contrary to "nothing happening" in this phase of the cycle, it's where integration occurs—where there is time and space for landing. Preparation for the next right thing happens. Meanwhile, we ensure we are adequately restocked for the next phase of the journey.

REPEAT

It wouldn't be a proper cycle if it didn't continue. It keeps moving—flowing—at both macro and micro levels. As patterns are revealed, our direction is refined and our awareness aligns. Just like the ebb and flow of breathing, a natural expansion and contraction reveals itself to be an inevitable part of The Change Cycle. It's not a moment but a part of the flow. It isn't a perfect circle, a bell curve, or even an infinity symbol. It's a moving, breathing, living state of being.

Awareness

Direction

Nonjudgmental Observation

"Re"cycle

Repeat

Choice unlocks The Change Cycle, and then we can get to work.

We don't have to look far to be reminded there are important lessons to be learned from every phase of the cycle. Even the nature of the changing seasons shows us there is a time for growth and a time to be fully in bloom. Spring ushers in new potential, and summer yields fruit. The leaves fall in autumn, and the winter quiets everything down, preparing for spring to arrive again. In her book *Birthdays of the Soul*, Barbara A. Bernard shares, "Our world and everything in it continuously grows and evolves. The changing seasons ground us in our understanding of the cycles of renewal. Even the harshest of winters is not permanent. As individuals, each of us changes over time" (Bernard 2014, 12).

When change is in progress and architecting our vision is in full force, all the tools in the world won't change anything on their own. The work of building, architecting, constructing, and translating a blueprint into something tangible is the task laid out before us. Choice is required to bring change to life.

We step into stretch, however difficult that is, and however narrow the stretch. We climb a rung on the permission ladder, which may help us stretch further. We shift our lens of perspective. In zooming in or out, we may realize we can climb another rung on the permission ladder, which allows us to stretch further. Returning to the tools for change, we remember this ARC of adaptability, resilience, and courage is already in us. We can lean into these tools to support us in further stretching, climbing the ladder of permission, and shifting our lens of perspective.

In all this, The Change Cycle fuels us. We return to awareness, choose a direction, observe, and reorient. The aliveness creates energy and momentum, propelling us toward the new:

- We hop on the bicycle and start pedaling.
- Instead of just swimming in the water, we ride the waves of change.
- Colors combine to create a masterpiece right in front of our eyes.

Kelly Kruse's most recent project is titled O *Mirabile* Mysterium—Oh Wonderful Mystery: Images of Creation. As she illuminates the biblical accounts of the creation story in visual form, she embraces an entirely new medium: mulberry paper. She cuts, tears, manipulates, and sculpts a material that at first might appear limiting. But as the paper absorbs water and color, it takes on a new life. It changes. It mirrors the miracle of creation itself, and Kruse believes it is proof that sometimes limitation can create spaces of flourishing. As she wisely shared with me, "There is no arrival point where you don't have to become, or you don't have to go through this process to change anymore. And I think that's what's beautiful." This is the beautiful, and humbling, reminder of change.

Change is multidimensional, shiftable, and transmutable. The more we can move and flow in and with the process, the more we can evolve with our journey. Rather than being about a fixed destination, real change is a dedication to a process. We can always shift our direction. When that happens, we make room for the next. Another unfolding, and the cycle continues. The ultimate gift is to align with the cycles of change. As we build our pathways forward, our journey reveals the life we most want to live.

PART III

CHANGING FOREVER

"The journey between what you once were and who you are now becoming is where the dance of life really takes place."

—BARBARA De ANGELIS

CHAPTER 10

It's Not a Diet; It's a Lifestyle

All I wanted were the french fries. Friends around me engaged in rousing conversation, but it was only muffled white noise to my ears. I sat there disconnected and preoccupied. I had promised myself I'd eat better, so I went on a diet. No fried foods and no carbs. Who knows, maybe I'd shed a few pounds? My morning routine had devolved from productivity to a few rounds of pressing the snooze button over the last few weeks. I could barely get through the day without an afternoon coffee. This diet might help give me the boost I need.

Hearing my name snapped me out of my haze. "Lisa. Earth to Lisa!"

"Sorry. Just trying to figure out what to order." *I should order a salad.* "Umm, I'll go with the chicken Caesar salad. Thanks."

Of course, the salad was perfectly fine. I just felt like an imposter. I sat there ignoring my friends and ordering a salad because I decided that's what I *should* be doing. The game of "what's been working for you these days?" felt like an endless cycle. My circle of friends and I had seen every diet under the sun: no carb, low carb, keto, high fat, no fat, juice cleanse, and broth cleanse. The diagnosis and the result were the same, as we temporarily addressed the need for a change and tried to get quick results. When something worked, it felt like hitting the jackpot. More often, each fad was a short-lived experiment that ended up leaving us exactly where we started. We're not alone. The global market for weight loss products and services was over $254 billion in 2021, anticipated to reach a whopping $377 billion by 2026 (Research 2021).

Regardless of the amount of time, money, energy, and effort we put into this yo-yo process, it didn't change two important facts: 1) I still just wanted the french fries, and 2) diets don't work. A 2020 study of over 21,000 participants and fourteen popular diet programs showed that even moderate effectiveness in weight loss after six months trailed off after twelve months (Ge et al. 2020). Why is the appeal so strong when the results are so poor? What makes us crave these results from quick-fix solutions found outside ourselves?

Diets don't work because they are often unconnected to sustainable, long-term change, nor do they take into account all the other factors of being a human that go into body health. Mentally, they feed into cultural programming that reinforces the idea our bodies are not accepted as they are. Physically, diets are predicated on spikes that shock our metabolism and hormones and often require a restrictive approach to food. This ultimately creates a greater obsession with food, which challenges our relationship with the whole process. The entire up-and-down act starts to feel like the elephant in the room. We don't want to talk about why it's not working but know we need something different.

Does this loop sound familiar? We know we want to change, and we make a rash decision to try something—anything—to get a different result. (Anywhere but here, right?) But in doing so, we can become obsessed with the choices we didn't make and what we could have chosen, and, filled with regret, we end up further away from something than we started.

This pattern doesn't just show up when discussing food and health. Even if it isn't trying the newest fad diet, we're often focused on the wrong things: spending time, energy, and resources putting Band-Aids on proverbial broken bones or continuously treating the symptoms of an unfulfilled life rather than figuring out where the problems lie. True and lasting change isn't a diet, it's a lifestyle. And the real difference is we must shift our relationship with change to create sustainability. In doing so, we adopt a mindset of *being in* change.

Elizabeth Benton's *Chasing Cupcakes* offers a crash course in sustainable transformation in every area of life. She writes: "When your thoughts reflect the way you want to be, you'll make a choice that creates the change you desire" (Benton 2018, 141). Her story of shedding the weight and debt she had been carrying offers insights into the thought patterns that can keep us trapped. Of the many valuable takeaways she offers, I was struck by two simple things she prescribes for overcoming an "all or nothing" mindset (Benton 2018, 162):

1. Self-awareness

2. Practice

As the old saying goes, practice makes perfect. Or, as I'll reframe it, practice means progress. What does practice, or progress, look like when it comes to change?

Throughout this exploration thus far, I have offered insights into tools and skills for navigating change. In the first chapter, "Change or Be Changed," I referenced a change management model that approaches change by utilizing three steps: Unfreeze, Change, and Refreeze. Sustainability in this change model means understanding we can, and should, honor all the cycle steps—they are valuable for different reasons and needed at different times. Sometimes water quenches our thirst. Other times, we need ice cubes of change to cool down our drink. There isn't an inherent better or worse: just the process. Living in the process reminds us we need to discover to change. We thaw, shift, and solidify again.

Sustainable change happens in cycles and flows and asks us to align our thinking with our tools and actions. Barriers to change are identified and broken down. The tools already existing within us provide support in approaching the unknown. As we move forward into action, our vision becomes more apparent. Skills to navigate change lead us to explore how stretch, permission, and perspective lead us straight into The Change Cycle:

- Awareness
- Direction
- Nonjudgmental observation
- "Re"cycle
- Repeat

The aim is progress, not perfection. It's about the journey, not the destination. Rather than viewing setbacks as failures, we view them as opportunities to learn as we explore our range of experiences more fully. As stories, anecdotes, and research have unfolded on this topic of change, I've noted what has been revealed: the quality, characteristics, and landscape of change are about living in alignment.

When we align ourselves, the right blend of five essential qualities creates a set of core values for a lifestyle of change. This offers us a clear pathway and a vital recipe for living in and embracing change. Here's the secret sauce—the recipe to **ALIGN**:

A—Authenticity

L—Learning

I—Intentionality

G—Gratitude

N—Nurturing

Through the following five chapters, exploring these core values will lead us to discover what it means to live in, with, and through change. I'll offer ways to practice strengthening and applying these core values as the pathways forward are designed and built step-by-step. ALIGN serves as a compass on the journey. It ensures we stay on course and provides valuable reference points to return to. Respecting the cycle and flow of sustainable change will highlight what each core value teaches us. Honoring different aspects of their application to our lives and experience, we explore these core values through the three various layers: self, process, and feelings.

When we honor ourselves, we recognize who we are and what we don't know. This offers us a place to start. In honoring the process, we continue to use tools and resources to strengthen new habits. Where feelings are concerned, we honor whatever comes up, acknowledging and holding space for it to be a part of the journey. We celebrate what it means to live in a mindset of changing and evolving. It won't always be easy, but remaining open and ready prepares us for whatever might come our way. As author and thought leader Adam Grant shares, "The right next move is the one that brings you a step closer to living your core values. In an unpredictable world, you can't make a master plan. You can only gauge whether you're on a meaningful path" (Grant 2022).

Although each of our journeys is a unique path to travel, it *doesn't* mean we have to do it alone. Shared experience is an important equalizer, and everyone has a unique experience with change. Others may not have the answers to your next steps, but they may be able to offer support on your journey. I can't imagine any scenario where I could plan, execute, and maintain control of every factor that gets me to where I think I want to go. And that's probably a good thing.

I can't possibly know how big I can dream if I'm limited to only what I already know. The stories of change that live all around us offer insights into how these tools, skills, and cycles of change emerge. They inspire us to aim higher than we might on our own.

Changing forever is a big prospect. Creating conditions that encourage ongoing change also supports a lifestyle of emerging and, eventually, becoming. Embracing these core, nonnegotiable values helps maintain balance, keeping us on track with our goals and visions. The next steps can be taken from a place of informed empowerment. Even if the next right move is a tiptoe forward, it's still a choice that takes us one step closer to where we want to be. This becoming is the gift of a life's journey.

CHAPTER 11

A—Authenticity: Our Truth

As I walked into the large, fenced-in area that Sunday morning, I didn't know what to expect. Although the sun shone brightly, the January day was still brisk. A fleeting, misty cloud formed just in front of my mouth as my breath met the cool air. My feet grazed the ground, and I left a slight poof of dust in my wake with each step. I had been instructed to go to the horse I felt most drawn to and be open to whatever interactions arose. Cimarron immediately caught my eye.

He was a leopard Appaloosa who came from a lineage of war horses. He stood proud and strong off to the side, next to the fence and away from the rest of the herd. I tentatively walked over, wondering what sort of greeting to offer such a majestic creature. *I guess I'll just try hello.* He seemed unfazed by my presence. He didn't seem to care whether I had chosen him. I felt a little ignored. Suddenly, as if he had decided it was time to get to work, he squared up right in front of me. I had never been that close to a horse before, and a hot wave of nervousness rose over me. As if sensing my hesitation, he simply closed his eyes and took a deep breath. Slowly, he let it out.

Oh! I think that's what he wants me to do too...

So, I did. I closed my eyes and took a deep breath. Unexpected tears flowed in solid waves, rushing down my cheeks. I felt the immediate urge to back away, find a solitary corner, and bury my face in my hands. Undeterred, Cimarron inched himself a bit closer. I stayed. Once again, he closed his eyes. I watched in awe as he took another deep breath in and slowly let it out. This dance continued, with him inching forward and asking me to breathe with him and me humbly responding. Eventually, he came so close I could almost feel the hairs of his nose touching mine.

I don't know exactly what I felt in those tears that day—other than the gift of being in a state of pure, authentic connection with a beautiful creature. I arrived searching for answers and insights on my next steps in life. Cimarron taught me I didn't—ever—have to be anything except for exactly who I was. Just being there together was enough. Knowing I was fully seen, felt, and accepted was a moment I will never forget.

The definition of authentic as "of undisputed origin or authorship" is quite different than its potential for application in our lives when defined as "a characterization, a descriptor of human personality, and the conception of an ideal" (Varga & Guidnon 2020). This definition offers the freedom to explore authenticity in what it means to be deeply human. Centuries ago, "being human" became more about the distinctive, unique traits we held as individuals than each of us existing as an anonymous piece of a larger social structure. Each of our choices shapes and informs the way we show up, and define ourselves, in the world. Fully embracing authenticity offers a pathway to truth, although it isn't always simple and requires commitment and work.

Or as Isabel Leonard puts it, "to be human is to be complex." She sighs through an easy laugh as she recounts to me her recent experience preparing for a new role. Over her fifteen-year career as an opera singer, she has brought countless characters to life. Industry demands require frequent travel, landing her on prestigious stages in cities around the globe. She's won three Grammy awards and has sung with the best in the industry, but none of that tells the story of authentically bringing her characters to life.

It would be easy to think performing is just jumping into role-playing a character. It's a world of pretend and make-believe with flashy costumes and showy sets brought to life under the bright lights of the stage. But that isn't her reality: "I'm not playing a character; I'm finding the thread of a real, flawed human and weaving it fully into the choices I make on stage. Rather than running from it, I have to be in it so deeply that I rediscover each moment, moment by moment."

Depending on the role, finding those threads can involve background research, reading the source material, studying physicality, and even learning special skills, whether a new dance style or playing the castanets. This unrelenting commitment shows up throughout Leonard's performance; her voice only does what it needs to do when she's authentically living out and fully embodying her character's sense of being.

The story might end the same way each time the curtain falls, but the experience changes each time the lights go up.

Leonard believes a certain magnetism comes from portraying her character's humanity, which inevitably draws from her own. Ignoring the responsibility to honor this authenticity would be a disservice to her art form and the integrity of what it means to be human. The truth is we are complex and multifaceted. As a single mother and successful artist, her work does not take place in a vacuum. It is informed by her understanding of life, loss, and love. Her work is a deep commitment to answering the question of what it means to portray a rainbow of emotions and find space for it all to be welcome. It's how she, as an artist, brings her craft to life and connects with an audience who experiences and interprets it in meaningful ways.

Authenticity is an unrelenting commitment to truth, lived out moment by moment.

Authenticity paints shades of gray in a world that feels more comfortable with black and white.

Authenticity asks for space in a cultural landscape where we're constantly being fed messaging that we need to change who we are to be accepted.

It means sometimes we make choices other people won't understand, choosing to listen to ourselves unforgivingly.

Years ago, this scenario was present for me as I sat uncomfortably in a chair, waiting to hear what an expert recommended

I do to address my jaw problem. With years of work in this field, he told me exactly what he suggested from a medical perspective. His recommended course of action was reconstructive jaw surgery. I've replayed this story in my mind many times, and endless questions flood my thoughts.

What would have happened if I had done the surgery? Would my life have taken a different path? Should I have listened to the expert? Will I have more problems later?

At that moment, authenticity meant being true to my instincts, intuition, and inner compass over the word of an expert, my mom, or anyone who might give me advice on the subject. And it taught me a few important things about this core value of authenticity.

Last chapter, I spoke about the sustainability of change which respects the cycles and flow of its process. To explore how these core values help us ALIGN with change, I'll break down the ways Authenticity, Learning, Intentionality, Gratitude, and Nurturing honor *self*, *process*, and *feelings*. What is revealed through these core values offers us insights into how to explore and strengthen them. Eventually, they become woven into the fabric of a lifestyle aligned with change.

Authenticity honors:	And is:
Self	Honest
Process	Genuine
Feelings	Vulnerable

To be *true to*, we have to be *in touch with*.

In *The Gifts of Imperfection*, Brené Brown shares "authenticity is a collection of choices that we have to make every day. It's about the choice to show up and be real. The choice to be honest. The choice to let our true selves be seen" (Brown 2022, 67). And that's not easy. It can feel like swimming upstream. Speaking our truth may go against what culture screams in our ears, reminding us of all the ways we need to change ourselves or urging us to conform to unattainable standards. Remember those whopping statistics about the weight loss industry? Get this: The beauty industry is projected to top $805 billion in sales by 2023, largely thanks to social media and digital marketing (Thomas 2020).

The fraught world of social media constantly challenges the ideal of authenticity. Presenting life in virtually curated, filtered snapshots and endless opportunities to scroll for more can result in dangerous comparisons, causing inner tension. Do we "keep up with the Joneses" and present an idealized version of ourselves? Or do we take a risk and dive into vulnerability by showing our authentic selves and telling our honest stories? Unsurprisingly, a study of over ten thousand Facebook users found those who displayed authentic self-expression were associated with a greater sense of well-being, when comparing idealized and authentic expression on the platform (Bailey et al. 2020). But this doesn't make the choice simple.

When author Lauren Bartleson started writing a book, she intended to pen a cautionary tale of "putting yourself out there" on social media. As a successful blogger, writer, and professional marketer, she loved connecting with people through words. In the world of social media, relevance is vital, so she chose what to write based on what was popular and would get people to the blog. Something always felt slightly forced about the approach, but it worked. She had over thirteen thousand followers on Instagram and an online presence that reached two hundred thousand people monthly. Over time, pervasive and painful negative comments got so bad she eventually had to shut it all down. No one had seen Lauren's struggles and the wounds she carried—anxiety, depression, and chronic health issues—because she had always presented a happy, smiling face.

Unsure of how to deal with the pain she was carrying, she turned back to words. To her surprise, her book changed course as she poured her heart onto the pages. She courageously shared her pain, her struggles, and her journey. *Behind the Facade: A Mental Health Memoir* chronicles her story. Being honest and raw was a choice she made to honor herself, but she also hoped sharing her story would help others struggling with their own challenges feel less alone: "Everyone wants a quick fix. They want to go to a life coach to change their lives. Or a therapist to answer all their questions. Those people aren't going to change your life. They can help you figure out what change needs to happen. But at the end of the day, it's on you."

Writing what was true and authentic became another form of healing. The book empowered her to be upfront about who she truly is and what she believes. Returning to social media has been a cathartic part of her process, as she worked to heal and reestablish that relationship. Sharing the journey of her book's creation was vulnerable. Celebrating its release to the world meant embracing all the pieces of her story, including the unfiltered truths of her silent struggles. Rather than hiding who she was, she made the choice to lead with authenticity.

Her goal is no longer relevance but resonance. She has been able to reach people she's never met who feel seen and understood through her words. The true story of Lauren Bartleson behind the facade isn't a collection of perfectly curated experiences. It's a moving reminder that being fully who we are is the most powerful medicine we can offer to the world.

Rarely is our experience one-dimensional. In moments of joy we may feel a twinge of pain. Moving forward sometimes means recognizing what we must leave behind. Through authenticity, we have a relationship with *"and"* rather than *"or."* Holding multiple, and sometimes conflicting, spaces isn't always comfortable or familiar. The challenge is to leave room for all it to be there, fully.

Honesty with self looks like a new mother who is overjoyed and full of more love than she could imagine AND has barely slept in days, quietly uttering the words, "I need help."

Being genuine with process surfaces in a boss who leads her team brilliantly AND, instead of pretending she has all the answers, will ask for help. She humbly works to figure out the problem by admitting, "I'm not sure I understand."

Vulnerability with feelings reveals itself in a woman who manages to hold it together on the outside but suffers from crippling anxiety and depression AND finds the strength to admit, "I'm not okay."

It's also grabbing on to the wild joys that come into our lives, understanding that with the highs come lows in respectful and ultimately beautiful cycles. In Chinese philosophy, this is yin-yang. Reflecting on the cycles of the day as seen in light and dark and movement and rest, the foundations for a deep and meaningful worldview arose. The yin-yang philosophy underlines three basic tenants (Wang, n.d.):

- The coherent fabric of nature and mind, exhibited in all existence.
- Interaction between the waxing and waning of the cosmic and human realms.
- A process of harmonization ensuring a constant, dynamic balance of all things.

Novelist and poet John Casey shares in *MERIDIAN: A Raw Thoughts Book*, "Yin and yang, fundamentally different yet symbiotic. I will never see one but for the other, as day has no meaning absent the dark, nor night without light, good without bad, right without wrong" (Casey 2021, 92). Authenticity is the embodiment of openness to inviting these balanced forces in, allowing them to inform how we show up in the world.

In the 2015 Pixar film *Inside Out*, Riley is an adolescent girl struggling with her emotions as she navigates a cross-country move from the Midwest to the West Coast, away from her friends and the only life she has ever known. As everything begins to fall apart, her emotions—Joy, Sadness, Fear,

Anger, and Disgust—work behind the scenes to keep things stabilized. Unable to successfully work together, disastrous consequences continue to unfold. The emotions cause poor Riley's understanding of who she is to suffer, and her sense of identity begins to crumble. Desperate to "fix" the problem, each emotion attempts a different solution. Joy, having spent most of her efforts squashing Sadness, eventually realizes that only by existing and forming memories together with Sadness can Riley be whole again.

The yin-yang in this display of authenticity, especially in the face of change, is a beautiful reminder that there is truth in being with all the parts of ourselves, feelings, and the process. Embracing authenticity is a stretch that's one of the essential parts of changing. Even when the stretch is far outside our comfort zone, cracks revealed can create unexpected ripples. Author and artist Christine Mason Miller believes, "When we focus our energy toward constructing a passionate, meaningful life, we toss a pebble into the world, creating a beautiful ripple effect of inspiration. When one person follows a dream, tries something new, or takes a daring leap, everyone nearby feels that energy, and before too long, they are making their own daring leaps and inspiring yet another circle" (Miller 2008, 21).

I often revisit my time in the arena with Cimarron. After my humbling lesson in connection, he modeled another important lesson of authenticity: congruence. He didn't care how I showed up that day. I could have been full of anger, fear, or disgust. To him, the important part was I fully embodied whomever I was, and whatever I felt, at that moment. I learned congruence does more than just reflect authenticity.

For horses, it is necessary to breed trust. Angry, fearful, or disgusted, at least I was being authentic.

Cimarron has now passed on, but his teachings still bubble up inside of me in moments when I'm faced with change. Exploring honest, genuine, and vulnerable authenticity through his eyes offered me a mirror to connection. He reflected the tools I already possessed, accompanied by an invitation to trust "me being me" was all any moment required. Much like our earlier exploration of the tools of change, my ARC—adaptability, resilience, and courage—followed me from that experience out into the world:

I started saying "no" to things when I didn't want to do them.

When asked for my honest opinion, I gave it—with kindness.

The next time a friend asked me how I was doing, I stifled the typical response of "fine." Unsure of whether she actually wanted to hear about how my world was falling apart, I quietly shared it had been a tough week. Instead of brushing me off, she leaned in a little closer. Her eyes closed as she calmly took a deep breath.

Tears filled my eyes. *Oh. I think that's what she wants me to do too...*

Remembering Cimarron, I soaked in the gift of this lesson that showed up as an important reminder. And you can bet I stopped everything to take a deep breath at that moment. I honored myself, the process of change, and my vulnerable feelings. The result? Once again, I was reminded I was enough, just as I am.

Carving out space for authenticity to emerge sets us up to align toward change as a way of life. We honor ourselves each time we speak our truth or model congruence. It's a stretch that sometimes pushes our edges. As we empower others with mirrors and reflections, perspective can shift. Ultimately, reclaiming the strength of this choice to be radically authentic gives others permission to do the same.

CHAPTER 12

L—Learning: Back to the Basics

I remember watching my younger brother take his first steps. Eight and a half years older than him, I understood how special this milestone was. I stole every moment I could to watch with rapt attention, observing how the process unfolded. First, he'd start pulling himself up. He'd hold on to something—anything—for support. Little by little, attempts to let go and balance would meet with success, usually followed by a fall.

Coos, "awws," and "oh nos!" would ensue. But, seemingly undeterred, he'd get up again.

Over time, a precarious balance on two feet led to an attempt to lift one foot off the ground. After countless attempts, falls, and getting back up again, eventually, it happened: He took his first step. Then another, and another, and another. Before too long, we were all happily running around chasing after him.

No one teaches a child how to walk. No one stands around and says, "Go ahead! Shift your weight balance. Lift your right foot! Transfer your weight as you take a step!" Most often we hear encouragements more like: "Come on!" or "You can do it!" or "Good job!" As outsiders to the process, we can provide guidance and support, but no one can learn something for someone else.

Learning is the second core value in our recipe to align with change—to support a lifestyle that remains resilient, adaptable, and courageous as our circumstances and environments shift. Learning is about acquiring new knowledge, but how to use, apply, and organize that knowledge is also a part of the learning process.

From our earliest moments, we employ a built-in survival mechanism to ensure we continue from moment to moment: the innate ability to learn. We are wired to use learning not only to survive but also to adapt, grow, and evolve. Showing up first as a built-in process (reflexes), this early ability to learn is innate. We have reflexively built-in behaviors that, along with the help of our caregivers, ensure we do indeed survive from one moment to the next. As helpless infants, we depend on our parents to ensure all levels of our well-being, as we are defenseless creatures who have no choice but to respond to the world around us.

Early learning happens as an experience of trial and error, coupled with curiosity and motivation. We lean on our continuous capacity to learn. If something doesn't work, we make a shift. We adjust. We continue to craft and hone our responsive decision-making process until we have reached some temporary destination, or at least have landed the desired result. Ideally, we also have the added benefit of lots of external support and encouragement from parents and caregivers.

This process is incredibly efficient: Our system finds something that works and then (wisely) stores it for future use. We store not only information about the result (what happened) but our brain also stores the learning process (how) and tries to apply it widely to as many situations as possible: walking, talking, eating, sitting, or even picking something up off the ground.

There's an incredible amount of both innovation and efficiency that accompanies these early learning processes. Although not reflexes, our learned patterns become reflexive responses—habits. Over time they solidify into more advanced techniques and patterns, which in turn become more habits. It's a gift we don't have to spend all our mental energy learning how to walk or talk each day. There wouldn't be room for much else in our brains.

As other factors come into play, things get a bit more complicated. Higher-order process thinking and various mental, social, and emotional factors start to affect and influence this learning process. In some ways, the stakes are high because the learning is happening rapidly, and it's exhausting. If you've ever seen a toddler fall asleep at the table while eating, you might understand! But in other ways, there's a simplicity to the learning process in these early years. The assimilation of information is constant, and how we use it to create a desired goal in our immediate surroundings is where our main focus lies.

As a child grows and matures, their learning never really stops. Their internal systems develop a conceptual framework for the vast amounts of input, processing, and assimilation of information so they don't have to think about how the learning process happens. And no doubt, these systems get more creative over time, trying to distill the aspects of various learning methods. We home in on styles, modes, and applied learning processes that can maximize our results. This happens faster and more efficiently than we can imagine: By age five, a child's brain is 85 percent developed. By age six, the brain starts working to determine what processes and patterns need to go so there continues to be room for new assimilation and learning.

Eventually, we use the incredible amount of information and processes available to us to make decisions and choices that move us closer toward our goals. As we age, we tend to lose some of the qualities of a more adaptive learning mode as we adopt and apply more specialized, focused thinking. As little ones, the goal might be excitedly and curiously moving our little toddling selves from one room to another. Our goal is to grab hold of our favorite toy or meet the thrill of going down a slide for the first time. As we get older, our goals get more specialized and focused, and the process can sometimes get a little complex.

Christine seemed to be born motivated and goal-oriented. At age eight, she organized the other neighborhood kids with the skills of a budding entrepreneur, mounting a lemonade stand at the end of the cul-de-sac. In Girl Scouts, she was the top cookie seller each year. She would plan her route to solicit door-to-door sales in her own neighborhood, as well as her grandmother's and aunt's too. As a teenager, she loved learning—reading, asking questions, and experimenting with creative business ideas—and was permanently relegating her family with stories of her big plans.

After graduating from college with a degree in marketing and a minor in business studies, she jumped into the workforce. A few years after leading her team in sales, she started an MBA program. She was focused and unstoppable. Although her program suggested forming a community and finding mentors, she didn't have time for that.

She spent all her spare time writing business plans and mapping out strategies. She rarely accepted invitations to join her friends for celebratory dinners or brunch on the weekends to catch up. When she finally did, her friends would ask about her big ideas. Her eyes would roll as she'd sigh and respond, "It's business stuff. I'm not sure you'd understand. I don't really have time to explain, anyways." Confused, her friends would shrug their shoulders. Eventually, they stopped asking, and the invitations stopped coming.

Although she used to play tennis and go to Pilates a few times a week, that too tapered off. There was no time for distractions. She poured her energy into the people she needed to help her achieve the next goal, but she wasn't always great about responding when they asked for something in return. Although she had set herself up for all the success in the world, she couldn't have foreseen what would happen just three months after her company launched in January 2020. As she struggled to shift her business online, she reached out to others for help but got few responses in return. And those who did respond apologized for not having the time to help. They were too busy managing their own challenges.

She didn't attend the course her friend recommended on moving your business online. She was convinced that wasn't what she needed. When a former MBA classmate asked if she wanted to brainstorm new business ideas, she kindly declined. She was sure spending her time on that kind of thing wouldn't do her any good now. Her choices had only further isolated her, and instead of being able to seek out support, learn, and grow, she told herself it was all doomed. Christine decided to cut her losses and look for a job with a marketing firm. It wasn't an easy decision, but there didn't seem to be a viable way to move her business aspirations forward.

She reflects on her difficult choice: "It was painful realizing that I was stuck with no options. Of course, it wasn't what I wanted, but there was nothing else I could do." She realized she had forgotten she still had much to learn.

If we want to use our ability to learn to help us change, we need to adapt some of these qualities to the process we have theoretically lost: curiosity, awareness, and open-mindedness. Christine had honed her focus so tightly it ultimately limited her capacity to grow. Rediscovering optimal learning qualities helps us change and adapt as we move forward. We seem to have inherently "known" how to do this when we were younger. But sometimes, things get lost—or left behind—along the way.

So what are the qualities of a more "youthful" approach we need to learn, or rather, relearn? Research done by Rachel Wu, George W. Rebok, and Feng Vankee Lin found there are distinct qualities younger children display in this early stage of "broad" learning. These qualities are (Wu et al. 2016):

1. "Open-minded input-driven learning:" learning new patterns, new skills, and exploring outside of one's comfort zone.

2. "Individualized scaffolding:" consistent access to teachers and mentors who guide learning.

3. "Growth mindset:" the belief abilities are developed with effort.

4. "Forgiving environment:" in which the child is allowed to make mistakes and even fail.

5. "Serious commitment to learning:" to master essential skills and persevere despite setbacks.

6. "Learning multiple skills simultaneously."

As we exit childhood, these qualities of broad learning tend to give way to those of what the authors' deem "specialized learning" when we move into a working or more career-oriented phase of our lives. There are clear benefits to this shift which allow us to pursue specific and advanced goals. The accompanying qualities of this specialized learning state also adjust. They end up looking like the opposites of those qualities in the broad learning category (Wu et al. 2016):

1. "Closed-minded knowledge-driven learning:" preferring familiar routines and staying within our comfort zones.

2. "No scaffolding:" no access to experts or teachers.

3. "Unforgiving environment:" high consequences for mistakes or failing, such as getting fired.

4. "Fixed mindset:" the belief that abilities are inborn talents instead of developed with effort.

5. "Little commitment to learning:" adults typically learn a hobby for a couple of months but then drop it due to time constraints and difficulty.

6. "Learning one (if any) skill" at a time.

We see that as our focus narrows and "specializes," so does our level of freedom. An open-minded and curious outlook gives way to close-minded, limited patterns. If we aren't careful, this focus reduction can affect *what* and even how quickly we learn.

For many years, neuroscientists believed new learning became more difficult—or even impossible—because our brain patterns had solidified once we reached a certain age. Today, we know an incredible amount more about our ability to learn and continue learning, thanks to the field of neuroplasticity. We can relearn and create new patterns throughout our lives.

Substantial research has been done over the past decades to deepen our understanding and application in this field of study. *The Brain That Changes Itself* by psychiatrist and psychoanalyst Dr. Norman Doidge was one of the early books in this field. In its follow-up, *The Brain's Way of Healing*, Dr. Doidge describes neuroplasticity as "the property of the brain that enables it to change its own structure and functioning in response to activity and mental experience" (Doidge 2015, xv). While it was once thought brain patterns were fixed once established, it's now understood the plasticity of the brain allows for rewiring. The establishment and creation of new synaptic patterns happens throughout life as we use them.

Neurons that fire together wire together.

There have been incredible discoveries of this phenomenon in the case of injury or trauma, where the brain has forged new neural pathways through rehabilitation. With a combination of care, attention, stimulation, training, and practice, doctors have helped patients walk again after accidents or regain speech after a stroke.

Outside of injury or trauma, anyone who has attempted a skill later in life has seen neuroplasticity at work. Learning a second language as an adult, picking up a musical instrument, or taking dance lessons are all easy examples. But as with any skill, learning requires a desire to engage, to seek out something new. As author Brian Herbert wrote: "The capacity to learn is a gift; the ability to learn is a skill; the willingness to learn is a choice" (Anderson & Herbert 2003, 532).

John Holt epitomizes the qualities of a life-long learner. He was a man who expressed that his only real problem was finding enough time to do the things he always wanted to do. Outside of his professional career as an educator and writer, he took up French and Italian at the age of thirty, skiing at thirty-one, cello for the first time at forty, water skiing at forty-seven, horseback riding at forty-eight, and violin at sixty. At the age of fifty-five, he wrote *Never Too Late: My Musical Life Story*, a memoir about his journey as a late-in-life musician. "We all have greater powers than we think; that whatever we want to learn or learn to do, we probably can learn; that our lives and our possibilities are not determined and fixed by what happened to us when we were little or by what experts say we can or cannot do" (Holt 197, 185).

To adopt learning as a core value that supports change, we must consider what it asks of us. What are the ways adopting and applying the tenants of learning to our lives can help catalyze important and distinct growth? Exploring this concept, we consider how learning shows up to influence our experience of the world and change.

Learning honors:	And requires:
Self	Curiosity
Process	Open-mindedness
Feelings	Motivation

In one of his whimsical drawings from his book *The Boy, the Mole, the Fox and the Horse*, published in 2019, artist and author Charlie Mackesy muses on how we might choose to approach the world: "I wonder if there is a school of unlearning[?]" The concept is not so far off from reality. In order to learn, we first need to unlearn—let go of past learnings, failures, and even successes—to approach something with the mindset of an explorative learner who matches the knowledge needed with their environment. In his book *Unlearn: Let Go of*

Past Success to Achieve Extraordinary Results, Barry O'Reilly talks about the value of "unlearning." It's an important skill to consider when "doing what you always did" doesn't yield the optimal results.

I remember the first time I had to drive on the left side of the road. I was in Ireland visiting a friend, and for almost a week, I walked to the wrong car door to get in. This didn't instill a lot of confidence in either of us. The process of doing something I knew how to do in an environment with entirely different rules and circumstances was different. I had to continuously remind myself, "Left is right, right is left," as I traversed the terrain.

Eventually, as we relearn, gaps are revealed. With a more motivated outcome in mind, we bring more choice to the learning process. O'Reilly shares: "Relearning is a process of experimentation to try new behaviors and take in new data, new information, new perspectives" (2018, 63). This relearning is where we can approach the process of learning with a sense of open-mindedness, curiosity, and motivation: a desire to not just acquire new information but also assimilate it. As we successfully use and apply these qualities, we can truly learn and grow.

Unlearning doesn't mean discarding or getting rid of information. Research suggests cognitive unlearning might be better defined as a process where subjects "reduce the influence of old knowledge" to create new knowledge and patterns of thinking (Grisold et al. 2013). It's not about erasing information off our brain's whiteboard store of learning, but about understanding what is needed. Discernment can be called upon to determine what information is no longer helpful. Other times information or experience needs to be added to the mix to allow for new learning.

This involves tools in The Change Cycle, namely awareness and a nonjudgmental approach toward our environment. Doing so can help prevent previous experiences from being projected onto current situations. Instead, we approach our future with a discerning viewpoint, determining what we want to take with us as we move forward.

As a classically trained musician, I became very familiar with this process of learning and unlearning. Each instance of creating music—whether a rehearsal, performance, or practice session—required the use of learned skills combined with an adjustment to manage the specific environment. A singer might need to change their pronunciation to be understood when performing in a space with live acoustics. Certain consonants might need to be exaggerated. A violinist might need to employ more separate rhythmic musical lines in that same live space. Even with these adjustments, the audience will still hear and interpret the sound as smooth and connected.

Any adjustment a musician might make takes into account their skill and experience. This requires leaning on the foundations of knowledge we may have acquired in the past. Paying attention and staying connected to our immediate circumstances is one aspect of this skill. Ultimately, this reflects the collaborative quality of music-making. Working in different settings and performing various types of music with diverse groups of performers ensures a musician never gets too stuck in their patterns.

Otto Scharmer reinforces this idea in *Theory U: Leading from the Future as It Emerges*. He offers a framework for seeing growth and learning in a new way, based on the idea of "presencing." What we pay attention to and *how* we pay attention to it influences what we can create (2009). This makes us aware of our blind spots and barriers, which are the patterns and habits preventing us from being able to move forward and, ultimately, change.

Here are three ways to get back to the basics and rediscover the qualities of learning that support change:

1. **Get curious:** I was out for a jog one afternoon and tuned in to an episode of *The Ezra Klein Show* titled "How Octopuses Upend What We Know About Ourselves." Although I didn't know anything about octopuses before that afternoon, I've now read books (including *The Soul of an Octopus* by Sy Montgomery), watched documentaries (*My Octopus Teacher*, anyone?), and brought my learnings into how I approach life. These fantastic creatures are true teachers, and even showed up earlier in this book in their spotlight on adaptability.

   Instead of making assumptions, turn thought patterns around into questions. What excites you? What makes you want to dig deeper? We can never go wrong if we follow our sense of curiosity. As educator Clay Bedford said: "You can teach a student a lesson for a day; but if you can teach him to learn by creating curiosity, he will continue the learning process as long as he lives."

2. **Be open-minded:** Learning as a quality, a habit, and a lifestyle requires a sense of open-mindedness to the approach. What needs to be unlearned? Do I need to relearn? What don't I know? Rather than being steeped in judgment, create opportunities for discernment. Perspective is critical here. To truly learn means acknowledging we don't know everything. Scientist Bill Nye reminds us, "Everyone you will ever meet knows something you don't" (UMass 2014, 24:35). Be a learning teacher and a teaching student, remaining open to all possibilities.

3. **Stay present:** Awareness and presence are vital in keeping our sense of motivation. What do we want to gain? What skill(s) can we learn from the people around us? How can being fully alive in any given moment help to illuminate our next steps? Continually listening—tuning in to the environment around us—can supply us with essential insights. We might even *feel* the excitement of something we are pulled toward. Maybe it's dancing. Or juggling. Or we are learning a new language.

Who says you can't teach an old dog new tricks? Dr. Norman Doidge's work and research seems to agree: "After the initial critical learning period of youth is over, the areas of the brain that need to be 'turned on' to allow enhanced, long-lasting learning can only be activated when something important, surprising, or novel occurs, or if we make an effort to pay close attention" (Doidge 2007).

Important crossroads emerge at any point where we can make a choice. We can choose the qualities of learning we want to adopt. Maintaining a curious, open, and motivated learning mindset allows us to continue through life more willing and able to change. Choosing where, and how, we want to apply these qualities can deepen and enhance our results. What would you do if you knew the sky was the limit and you could learn, be, or even *change* anything? It's never too late.

CHAPTER 13

I—Intentionality: The Art of the Pivot

I had done it. I landed an interview for a job with a Commercial Real Estate firm. There was just one problem: I didn't know anything about real estate. The position was entry-level, but to say I felt less than qualified would be an understatement. Unsure of the next steps in my professional career, I just knew I needed a full-time job. I wanted to move into a different industry and was open to learning new skills. I knew this would require a pivot. Reaching out to friends and family, I scoured my networks and secured this opportunity.

My hands felt clammy as I walked into the office for the interview that day. Wearing my favorite red heels and a grey summer suit at least made me look confident, even if I didn't feel it. I wasn't sure how to approach the interview. In college, I majored in music. Performing may not have been in my professional future, but I learned invaluable skills. Following my undergraduate studies, I worked at a daycare school teaching music part-time, as a server at a bar, and then as a live-in nanny. Each time I highlighted the skills that could set me up for success in a new field. Pivot once, pivot twice, and pivot again.

In some ways, this situation was not that different. I *did* know what I brought to the table. Musicians are skilled collaborators and good friends with organized structure—hello, practicing! I had a dynamic personality and excellent communication skills. Whether in the restaurant or working with kids, years of working "on the floor" had definitely taught me a thing or two about listening, reading people, and working efficiently. Even if I didn't have direct experience, I did have the skills needed to do the work. I was eager. I knew I could succeed.

I got the job. Six years later, I amassed incredible knowledge about an entirely new industry. I made meaningful professional connections and forged lasting, influential relationships. This had been an intentional and successful pivot, and it wouldn't be my last. Setting the stage, this skill prepared me for the next jumping-off point I would encounter in my life, whenever that might come along.

Following Authenticity and Learning, Intentionality is the next core value in living a life aligned with change. Defined by Defined by *Oxford Languages* (2023) as "*deliberate or purposeful*," being intentional is more than simply "doing." In the world of change, intentionality in action is "directed choice." It becomes an art. There is great power in choosing to choose.

This concept is deceivingly simple. It requires understanding the types of choices we can make and knowing the difference between reacting and responding. Reaction is a natural process, but a relatively unconscious one. Often, reactions are impulsive. We can be grateful for this evolutionary tool of reaction for efficiency. It's an indicator our system is tuned to our environment. Its imperative automatic reaction removes our hand from a hot surface rather than waiting to think about how to respond. It allows us to adapt—a skill very needed when navigating change. Our system isn't concerned with sustainability and longevity when it is in this reaction mode. Its foremost concern is working through the current task, issue, or question at hand.

Response, however, appears as something different. A response is more conscious and intentional. The answer supplied to a choice, question, or situation holds a different quality. A thought-through response is more present and connected, and our decision is often more resolved. What is the difference between reacting and responding? Intentionality.

Growing up in a small town in the Midwest, Emily had taken her upbringing for granted. Her parents used to drive her crazy with their one-liners and adages. Her dad was handy around the house and had an incredible knack for being able to grab the right tool for the job. Sometimes it felt like he had a stash of tools in each room of the house. He was known for saying things like "Measure twice, cut once!" Whenever she asked him for advice, he'd say, "Check in with your guts. What are they tellin' you to do?"

Her younger sister had tattled on her during a particularly memorable family dinner. Right in the middle of passing potatoes, she blurted out she had seen Emily walking with a boy after school—holding hands. Embarrassed, Emily's face turned red as soon as the words came out of her sister's mouth. Her eyes darted around, and the heat of her anger rose as she opened her mouth to respond. As if able to read her mind, she remembers how her mother gently caught her eyes with a knowing glance. "Think before you speak, Emily. Once the words are spoken, they can't be taken back." Huffing away from the dinner table that night, she recalls the tears that stung her eyes. But she was grateful she didn't say something she regretted.

Years later, she realized intentionality had been modeled in almost everything her parents did. Their responses included time and space to consider all sides of a scenario. Whether a home improvement project or giving advice, the result was always the same. Emily felt a constant invitation to reconnect with intentional choices modeled in many moments and lessons growing up.

Emily found herself revisiting her parent's words in countless scenarios throughout her adult life. Whether struggling to find a solution at work or dealing with her kids, she was reminded she had a choice. She could always take space and lean on an opportunity to consider what she needed. She requested "think breaks" at work when she was stuck on an idea. She would tell her husband they needed to "take a beat" if things got heated. They could get clear on what they needed and wanted to say. Honoring their needs as individuals carved pathways to deeper and more meaningful choices and connection as a unit. It wasn't always easy, but they had never met a problem they couldn't approach. Sometimes beginning with tears, small arguments would often end in rolling fits of laughter. Rarely did they reach a resolution without the two of them sharing a warm and meaningful embrace.

Whether at work or home, being present in the moment was critical. Identifying where things stood at any given moment offered an opportunity to embrace intentionality. Emily still believes this was one of the biggest lessons of her life. "I didn't realize how important it was to be sure I knew what I was choosing in any given moment. And I certainly didn't appreciate it at the time. Now, I can't imagine going through life without this approach."

As children, we are encouraged to "count to ten" before responding to counteract our anger. Creating some space often works as it allows the initial wave of emotion to subside. "Taking a deep breath" is not just anecdotal in affecting the quality of our response. Our parasympathetic nervous system is built in to help calm or recenter us after being activated. This entire system is directly accessible through the activation of the vagus nerve. Any guesses about one of the simplest ways to activate the vagus nerve? Intentional breathing. Helpful research has shown deep breathing increases vagal nerve activity, measured by heart rate variability, and improves decision-making (De Couck et al. 2019).

In her book *A Minute to Think*, Juliet Funt speaks about actively creating what she calls "white space." White space occurs anytime we step back and take a strategic pause. More than just a healthy habit, it's a valuable tool for whatever outcome we wish to reach. She shares: "Call it gap, buffer, slack, or margin, allowing white space between our endless doing makes everything better" (2017, 20). What arises in this space creates the opportunity for potential and intentionality.

This concept of encouraging intentionality by creating time and space extends to Funt's hourglass method for decision-making. Instead of funneling sand, decisions are funneled through an hourglass shape. The inevitable slowing down in the middle offers a space—a "strategic pause"—between what she calls a "flash response" and a "considered response" to a question. In this strategic pause, there is an opportunity to investigate our desires, goals, and intended outcomes. Although our eventual response might ultimately be the same as our initial "knee-jerk" reaction, there is a different quality to having truly chosen our actions. Words attributed to psychiatrist and author Viktor Frankl offer important insights on this idea: Between stimulus and response, there is a space. In that space is our power to choose our response. In our response lies our growth and our freedom. "Choosing to choose" is intentionality in action.

Intentionality is a significant core value in all aspects of our lives. From how we engage with others to how we spend our time, our choices reflect who we are. Every choice we make is a step toward building the future we inhabit. Inviting space and being present offers pathways connecting our choices and actions in a way that enhances our experience.

As we deepen our understanding of what it means to show up and choose intentionally, we are reminded of what that choice offers us in return. As we return to building and strengthening a set of core values to ALIGN with change in our lives, we recognize the impact intentionality offers.

Intentionality honors:	And invites:
Self	Space
Process	Presence
Feelings	Connection

Occasionally there can be a false sense of urgency or fear and anxiety when it comes to decision-making, especially when we worry we might make the "wrong" choice. In her paper titled "Hard Choices," philosopher Ruth Chang discusses the challenge of making these "hard choices." Now, we aren't talking about choices like "Which dessert should I choose?" or "What do I wear tonight?" Although those can certainly be hard choices! Instead, these hard choices weigh heavily because the results of these choices have more substantial outcomes. The choices we make influence and define us: decisions like who to marry, what career to pursue, or where to live.

Under these higher-stakes circumstances, the traditional tools for making choices don't apply. Gathering more information may not make the decision simpler. The result of each option can't be measured, and even a list of pros and cons doesn't necessarily help shed light on how to move forward.

Chang describes these choices as "on a par." One choice isn't inherently right or wrong, better or worse. The result of choice simply yields different outcomes. She argues commitment is required in these instances. Making a decision based on desire and will, our *intention* is the factor allowing us to make these hard choices (Chang 2017).

Committing to our choices can also be reinforced when we tune inward. Our body offers an incredible tool for feedback and direction. How do decisions feel in your body, physically? Do your choices and patterns align with who you are? Or, as Emily's father might have asked: What are your guts telling you to do? Sometimes the answers to these questions become the backdrop for the biggest changes in our lives as the power of intention and choice resonates throughout our entire system.

From a fast-tracked career in finance to the bright lights of the Broadway stage, Jessica Vosk's journey epitomizes the art of the pivot, and the intentionality it took to get there. The choice to pivot wasn't part of a long-term plan. The need to make a change came directly from her gut. "For me, it happened within my body. My body actually had a stress and traumatic response via panic attacks and anxiety when I was working the finance job. My body basically said to me, 'You're not supposed to be here' and 'This isn't what you love to do. Why are you not doing what it is that you love to do?'"

Her desire to perform was simple and clear, but the decision to leave a lucrative and successful career path in finance was not. A pivot like this meant not only a career change but a lifestyle change. The loss of a regular paycheck, health care, and 401K would be a complete shift. There wasn't a rule book, nor were there mentors she could look up to for support as she paved her pathway forward. Everyone from her parents to colleagues and friends suggested it was the worst decision she could make. Starting from scratch meant truly reinventing her path. "I had to throw all that out the window and completely rely on myself and my instincts and my gut, telling me that

I had to do something else. That I would never quite truly be happy unless I took a leap of faith and did the thing that I was passionate about."

The glossy, polished version of her success story fast-forwards to the Broadway stage. Night after night, Jessica Vosk defied gravity as the iconic green witch Elphaba in the popular musical *Wicked*. She landed the leading role four years after making her Broadway debut in *The Bridges of Madison County* at age thirty, then performing in *Finding Neverland*, with other engagements along the way. Focusing solely on these incredible accomplishments does highlight her outcomes and success in pivoting. Yet, Vosk describes her favorite moments of the journey as the moments no one saw. The stress and the tears, the pounding down doors, and the constant showing up for the chance to be heard all made her stronger.

Each choice she made was steeped in intentionality. She gave herself six months, logging in daily hours at her finance desk between 8 a.m. and 6 p.m. Waiting around all night until a jazz club opened, she would go to open mic nights. She tapped in relentlessly, writing her name on the list to perform each night. Although she never knew if she would get the chance, she tried over and over again.

In between odd jobs, and babysitting many of her friends' kids, she would audition every day. Her perspective shifted focus as she leveraged each opportunity she was given. Each closed door just meant working harder to find a new one that could be opened. She asked questions and with each one, would discover new pathways. Recognizing she did not have all the answers, she seized every opportunity to learn from directors, colleagues, and other performers.

Stretching herself, she voluntarily moved into spaces of discomfort. Repeatedly, she heard "no." Nothing was wasted, but there was no sugarcoating the difficulties she faced. Still, she took every step with intention. She gave herself shameless permission to pivot, try, fall, and fail. For all her successes, she's still not where she wants to be. "There is something to the fact of 'slow and steady wins the race' when it comes to building the life that you truly want."

As for today? Standing in the wings backstage waiting to step out into the lights, Jessica Vosk's body still speaks to her. Shaky with adrenaline and her heart racing, her nerves are all still there. But unlike the sense of doom that accompanied the messages before, her body is now in alignment with her choices. She gratefully and intentionally reconnects in those moments. "I actually thank God, thank the Universe, that my nerves exist because otherwise I shouldn't be doing this. You know, it's kind of like the butterflies in your stomach are trying to tell you, 'Yes. This is exactly where you're supposed to be.'"

In life, a pivot is an essential tool of intentionality. Requiring the tools of change—the ARC of adaptability, resilience, and courage—helps us see new possibilities and illuminate opportunities along our path. In some cases, pivots require us to stretch as we shift gears to move far and fast. In other cases, we don't have to abandon where we have come from to move forward. We can lean into permission and perspective to discover possible pathways to change we didn't even realize were possible.

In the professional sphere alone, most individuals will change jobs an average of twelve times throughout their working life. Personally, countless pivots require a change of direction. Change following a linear path is not always possible and is highly improbable. Pivoting isn't the exception to the rule; it is the name of the game. This process is a cycle of change through which we design our path forward. As Jay Samit, author of *Disrupt You!*, said, "Pivoting is not the end of the disruption process, but the beginning of the next leg of your journey" (2015, 128).

The goal is to make choices that focus more on what we want to do and bring us closer to who we truly want to be. Intentionality asks us to take the time and space to tune inward and listen to our bodies. This ensures we never lose our sense of "why" as we make choices that result in inevitable change. Even when we aren't sure exactly where we want to end up, exploring the art of pivot is an incredible tool of intentionality.

Far from simply an ideal, intentionality as a core value can be cultivated by:

1. **Creating space and taking time:** Take a few deep breaths. Literally. Whether it's a breath, thought, word, or action, a "strategic pause" creates the opportunity to make more intentional choices. Even if a sliver of space or time is created, this is a habit for consistently providing a moment to reassess—stretching or shifting perspective if needed. Over time, this space will grow. Whether Emily's "think breaks" or Juliet Funt's "strategic pause," consider what techniques help you take more time and create more space.

2. **Choosing to Choose:** Whether making hard choices or simply making a more engaged choice, committing to the act changes the result. Give yourself permission. Start small. Choose something where the stakes aren't quite as high—the age-old "What's for dinner" works well—and work your way up to the feeling of commitment that comes from a fully empowered choice.

3. **Reframing regret:** Let go of the binary nature of "right" and "wrong." Intentionality is about recognizing choices are choices. Rather than dwelling on what happened in the past, focus on what might take you toward your next steps. If that means making another change, take a deep breath and begin from where you are.

Like with many tools, ideas, and core values, intentionality takes practice and reinforcement. Celebrate by dancing around the room. Discuss hard topics with your neighbors or coworkers. Share challenges with your family and friends. Hold yourself accountable with notes or reminders.

At first, it may feel like a stretch, but over time, intentionality becomes woven into how we live and engage with the world. There is no rush, race, or prize for the number of goals we achieve in life. We hold the keys to our future and can choose at any point. Leading with intention is always an option.

CHAPTER 14

G—Gratitude: The Constant Gardener

It's no secret to anyone who knows me that I don't exactly have a green thumb. The few plants I have in my home are primarily succulents because, to the best of my intentions, I can't seem to keep anything else alive. The one exception is a beautiful sansevieria sent to me as a housewarming gift by one of my close friends. Initial excitement at the large box's arrival at my doorstep quickly gave way to a momentary panic: I wasn't sure I could keep it alive. My knowing friend just laughed. She considered the plant carefully when she picked it out. She ensured I could manage it perfectly. Directions included "water only when completely dry" and "feed once every six months"—read: hard to kill. It was made for someone, like me, who hasn't quite taken to the art of gardening. I'm proud to report that it's earned the title of "longest-living houseplant" to date.

Personal horticulture shortcomings aside, along with the occasional worry I have, in fact, overwatered, I felt the addition of "life" that had been breathed into my new space. My friend had gone out of her way to offer me a gift that would both enhance my home and stretch me out of my comfort zone. I was overcome with gratitude. This gift was a reminder someone saw—really knew—me and took the time to ensure I felt cared for. The act itself was simple but also genuine and profound.

Gratitude is the quality of being thankful, a readiness to show appreciation for and return kindness. Following Authenticity, Learning, and Intentionality, Gratitude is the fourth of the core values for living a lifestyle that supports change. Perhaps not entirely ironically, the "G" in ALIGN is silent. Gratitude has been a sometimes quiet but ultimately pervasive presence in our world. Gratitude provides important context to a sustainable life of changing, reminding us it isn't always about doing. Instead, it offers the opportunity to melt into the space of feeling, sensing, and appreciating.

Gratitude isn't "new" to the scene. The concept has deep roots in theological, moral, and philosophical teachings, but only in the past few decades has it been brought into psychological realms of focus. In his introduction to *The Psychology of Gratitude*, Robert Emmons comments: "in the history of ideas, gratitude has had a long life span, but in the history of psychology, a relatively short past" (2004, 3). He notes gratitude doesn't appear in some quintessential literature on emotions, neither in the *Encyclopedia of Human Emotions* nor the *Handbook of Emotion*, and only once in the *Handbook of Cognition and Emotion*, all published within the last twenty-five years. A few short decades later, a quick book search with the word "gratitude" on Amazon yields over seventy thousand results—not only books but also journals and daily guides—which all focus on cultivating gratitude as a powerful and altering emotion, fulfilling state of mind, and meaningful life choice.

Gratitude isn't just a trend that is socially popular in personal wellness realms today. It's considered a factor that contributes to the health and well-being of a society, offering meaningful relational connections. As a response to and motivator of moral activity, gratitude supports more prosocial behavior in our world. Prosocial behavior can be described as "any behavior that is intended to benefit another" (Dunfield 2014). In benefiting others, we help tend to their needs, whether it will directly benefit us or not. When we don't receive any direct benefit, our actions in support of others in our community are considered altruistic or charitable.

Biological evidence of this community support—give and take—also arises in the natural world. Reciprocal altruism "occurs between unrelated individuals when there will be repayment (or at least the promise of repayment) of the altruistic act in the future" (Trivers 1971). It's a concept studied in birds, fish, and primates, with one study finding chimpanzees were more likely to share their food with another chimpanzee who had helped groom them that day (de Waal 1997). Scientists Robert Axelrod and William D. Hamilton elaborate on this concept: "The theory of evolution is based on the struggle for life and the survival of the fittest. Yet cooperation is common between members of the same species and even between members of different species" (1981).

Birds flying in V-formation take turns leading and following, pairing up, and matching the time in each position during the grueling migration process (Voelkl et al. 2015). Species of cleaner fish swim into the mouths of larger host fish, playing an essential role in biology: they are almost entirely immune to being eaten by the host fish. Both mutual dependence and a sense of community support show up in these real-life examples from the natural world.

The 2000 film *Pay It Forward* shares the story of seventh grader Trevor, whose social studies teacher gives an assignment to implement a plan that would "change the world." Trevor launches a "pay it forward" plan: Rather than paying someone back for a good deed, a favor is performed for three others in return. His young mind's ambitious project starts a connected branch of good deeds that reaches thousands of people.

The term "helpers high" was coined in the 1980s, noting the distinct onset of positive emotions which followed acts of selfless service (Dossey 2018). More than just a feeling, this state is also associated with increased immune function and a lower level of stress hormones. Gratitude has become more of a focus of research and studies over the past decades, and results from various studies confirm gratitude has clear, consistent, and significant effects on our health, happiness, and well-being:

- A 2015 study on gratitude practices as a tool for those seeking mental health support concluded gratitude writing practices contributed to significantly better mental health four and twelve weeks after the writing activity ended (Wong et al. 2016).

- Ongoing gratitude practices have been seen to reduce stress and inflammation and even help support better sleep (Jans-Beken et al. 2019).

- Gratitude verbally expressed between romantic partners not only improved interactions but also was a predictor of significant improvement in relationship quality six months later (Algoe et al. 2013).

Gratitude connects us with others and deeper within ourselves, ultimately affecting our psychological happiness, health, and well-being. It can appear unexpectedly, as simple as a small act, a few words, or a knowing look. And sometimes a simple, small act changes everything.

My friend and I had just finished lunch on a beautiful late spring afternoon. We hadn't seen each other for a while but fell back into laughter and conversation like no time had passed. After repeated annoying vibrations, I glanced down at the buzzing timekeeper on my wrist. I had missed a call I needed to take and started getting text messages from my colleague at work. It had gotten late, and I had overscheduled my afternoon. The side of my mouth rumpled in at one corner, and I sighed, knowing I'd have to rush off to get to my next appointment on time.

Although I tried to catch his eye, the server didn't seem to be paying attention. I grumbled under my breath as he finally saw my waving arm. He brought the check, and I hurriedly paid. Leaning over to grab my jacket and bag, I quickly checked to ensure I had everything I needed. My watch buzzed again, and as I looked down to check it, I felt my friend's hand land gently on my arm. "I'm so grateful we're friends."

The words froze me for a moment as my eyes filled with tears. I'd known this friend for over twenty years. Of course, I felt the same way. But how often did I take the time to reflect on it? Had I openly expressed it to her? What did it mean to truly feel gratitude?

She leaned in and gave me a big, unhurried hug. "I know you have to go. Thanks again for making time on such a busy day."

I paused and smiled as I pulled her in for one more embrace. I felt my body soften, the worries about my meeting melting away. I hate to think what would have happened if I hadn't taken that moment to notice and stay present. Her unexpected expression of gratitude left me on a high for the rest of the day. This one small exchange gave me an important example of the way I could choose to show up in my world. No matter how busy I was, it was important to hold space for gratitude. Even starting small plants a seed that inevitably grows. I now try to express my gratitude as often and authentically as possible.

I met Barb when she was embarking on a new chapter of her life. She was in her late forties, with two sons in high school. She had gotten married right out of college and initially thought she might look for a job once the children were in preschool. But when her youngest son was diagnosed with autism at age three, she knew she was needed at home. Although the choice was obvious, it wasn't always easy.

Her husband didn't take the news of the diagnosis well and would come home from work irritable and impatient. Barb would encourage her husband and youngest son to bond by setting up a puzzle or game. Inevitably a short-lived interaction would end with her son running to her crying and her husband storming out of the room. As the years wore on, their marriage slowly eroded. After a painful divorce, she was unsure how to move forward: "I spent so much time focusing on all the things that weren't right that I forgot to notice all the good things. The things that I could be grateful for."

She took notice, deciding to turn as many interactions as possible into grateful ones. The ideas sprouted spontaneously. She began thanking people for helping her, holding a door, or just sharing a smile. At first, she'd get a few sideways looks, and occasionally she'd be asked, "What makes you so happy all the time?"

She'd give a sly smile, saying, "I guess life's too short not to notice."

Over time, her gratitude increased to more specific and intentional expressions, including volunteering for the food pantry and organizing the "thank you lunch" at her kids' school. Soon, her entire world seemed to beam with technicolor images. She had more capacity to show up and be present at home, brought a smile to everyone's face, and was the resident morale-booster at work. As laughter filled their home, her relationship with her kids became more and more meaningful. She noticed even her sons had started to thank her, and other people, more often. Her gratitude became a contagious tool that helped heal some of her painful moments, allowing her to embrace unexpected shifts with a sense of appreciation.

It can be easy to bypass the nature of gratitude as a core value for its results. "Being grateful" is more than just an ideal. As a core value, gratitude offers a space to deepen and grow. We explore what it means to align with gratitude, recognizing what is needed to allow it to show up and enhance our lives.

Gratitude honors:	And requires:
Self	Kindness
Process	Presence
Feelings	Appreciation

Tending to gratitude as a practice, a habit, and a mindset is like tending to a garden. It requires us to plant the seeds, feed and nourish them, and care for them as they grow. There are inevitable moments when finding gratitude doesn't feel possible. In a culture where toxic positivity—bypassing the feeling, and showing, of genuine emotion—is offered as a substitute, we may need to extend ourselves a bit of grace. Gratitude isn't about being happy at all costs. Instead, it's about accepting and appreciating whatever arises.

In my own experience, I started to refer to this phenomenon as "uprooted gratitude:" a choice to embrace deep gratitude even when it's hard to see the light at the end of the tunnel. The possibilities are endless when celebrating small moments each day. Whatever tomorrow might bring, each day is new.

In *Cultivating Gratitude: A Guided Journal for a Positive Mindset*, Beth Bunchman shares: "Gratitude is more than a feeling of appreciation or thanks. More than a returning of kindness. And more than giving recognition to the sources of those kindnesses. Gratitude is also about seeing obstacles and struggles as an opportunity for growth—a gift of possibility and an affirmation of potential" (2016, 26).

Krissy's life changed instantly when she discovered she had a brain tumor at twenty-seven. She experienced several days of extreme nausea and feeling generally "off," but didn't find out about her tumor until she had seizures for several days. A trip to the emergency room came with the diagnosis, with emergency brain surgery scheduled a few days later. She bluntly reflected, "That first week was the worst of my life." Post-surgery she would experience double vision, confusion, and even more nausea. Following her surgery were the next steps of the journey, including inpatient rehab, egg-freezing (which took place before beginning a month and a half of radiation and chemo pills), then a year's worth of monthly chemo pills. Her healing was not just her life but also became her survival mode.

In the few days before her emergency surgery, she experienced what she refers to as her "live funeral," as people from all walks of life came out of the woodwork. The sobering news meant everyone faced the shock and the possibility she might not survive the surgery. From elementary school classmates to old boyfriends, people gushed reflections of what she meant to them. Often, they would reminisce on their relationship. Although it felt strange, she knew most people didn't get this kind of opportunity. It became a catalyst for a completely new mindset as she shifted her perspective toward life.

She realized how much she had taken for granted. There had been little personal and professional growth in her life. She "lived for the weekends" and would spend most Sundays nursing a hangover from too much fun the night before. She had always loved her family but her gratitude for them, especially her mom, shifted in a way she couldn't have imagined. Her family had sustained her through the most challenging time of her life.

Krissy's practice of gratitude showed up partially for her survival and sanity. It also brought out the person she didn't realize she was: supremely positive, extraordinarily passionate, and motivated. Initially, her goal was to make a daily gratitude journal entry, but she soon challenged herself to find three "little wins" each day. Amid her healing journey, these small moments of celebration—gratitude—were sustaining. They gave her a way to appreciate life. Now, she *thinks* in little wins. "Ding!" she laughs. "There's another one!"

Krissy did get a portion of her brain tumor successfully removed and is living life to the fullest. She attributes her ability to cultivate a life full of gratitude and intention as one of the biggest reasons she can, and will, continue to navigate change. The seeds of gratitude planted in the harshest conditions bloomed into a lifestyle that sustains and supports the person she is today. She is now living a life she is proud of.

She wrote a book about her journey, *My Brainstorm*, that offers her bright and humorous outlook amidst her frightening experience. In her spare time, she works to advocate for finding a cure while helping address another issue she faced in her journey: fertility. She was suggested to freeze her eggs. Told that it can be unsafe for women with cancer to carry a child while twenty-seven and single, Krissy started dedicating time and resources to finding a way for surrogacy to be financially supported for cancer patients.

She reflects with an easy sigh and an infectious smile: "If I have the surrogacy, if I find a man, if I have kids—I already know. At dinner every night, I'm going to ask everyone at the table, 'What were the three little wins of your day?' Because I think it can help them keep a positive mindset toward life, even when things suck."

The previous research on negativity bias and neuroplasticity is a sobering reminder gratitude may not start as the most natural habit. Yet the power of choice can have a lasting influence on our brain chemistry. When we rewire our brain to find the "good," we shift our ability to embrace change, whether in a tiny decision or one that ends up being life-altering.

Here are a few tangible practices that can allow us to plant, seed, and cultivate gratitude that can start at any point:

1. **Find (and celebrate!) "little wins":** As Krissy discovered in her journey, identifying a few "little wins" each day can be a powerful way to plant the seed of gratitude in our life and experience.

2. **Keep a gratitude journal:** A gratitude journal is a great way to chart and reinforce the loop of gratitude. If you're overwhelmed about where to start, treat yourself to a guided journal or daily guide that can assist with prompts.

3. **Write a letter of gratitude:** It doesn't matter if you write the letter to yourself or someone else, and it doesn't even matter if you send it—although that's good too. Part of the practice of cultivating gratitude is using words and engaging in a way that reinforces our connection to others.

4. **Express gratitude or "thanks" to others:** As Barb noticed, expressing gratitude out loud can begin rewiring our capacity for gratitude and influence others tangibly.

5. **Reflect on moments of sharing and feeling gratitude:** Just *thinking* about them is a start. Earlier, I referenced the proven positive effects that kindness, gratitude, and generosity can support, but fascinating research has also proven simply *thinking* about these acts stimulates the same part of the brain as actually doing them (Dossey 2016).

Choose a regular time of day when you're not distracted. Be honest about when it's easy to set aside time and when it would be easy to find an excuse not to do it. Start small and aim for once a day. Being realistic about your patterns and limitations can help set up success. The practice of gratitude is a conscious choice that starts with our thoughts. As William James was quoted, "The greatest revolution of our generation is the discovery that human beings, by changing the inner attitudes of their minds, can change the outer aspects of their lives" (Johnson 2004, 127).

As with building new habits and strengthening skills, practicing gratitude takes consistency. We may not always be in the mood or have the ability to find gratitude, but in those moments we can also learn to offer ourselves a little grace. All these are choices we can learn to make by tapping in. We commit to being patient with ourselves and the process, and stay present enough to notice what we might need to alter to feed and nourish best. Instead of standing idly by and hoping presence will come, we practice and continually choose to be ripe ground, a carefully cultivated space for presence to bloom.

In attempting to tend to my own gardens, I quickly blamed the plants. They were high maintenance or "too picky" about their conditions. I didn't know what kind of plant food they required and wasn't sure how to find out. But it wasn't about the plants or what they needed to grow and thrive. We all need different things to ensure we bloom and reach our full potential. It reminded me of this quote by inspirational speaker and author Alexander Den Heijer: "When a flower doesn't bloom, you fix the environment in which it grows, not the flower" (2018, 22).

We may not be in control of many aspects of our lives, but we can look at the environment we create to support our goals, dreams, and direction. As we tend to our gardens as a practice and a habit, they will eventually yield growth. The same is true for us. We set our environment, and we seed, we plant, and we bloom. Eventually we grow, shift, and change. To begin, choose just one act of gratitude. Start today.

Fleuris là où tu es plantée: Bloom where you are planted.

CHAPTER 15

N—Nurture: Becoming

My nana was one of my favorite people, so it isn't surprising her home was one of my favorite places to be. It was like someone had bottled up all the magic in the world and deposited it straight into those walls. There were special treats in glass jars we could only get off the bottom shelf of the pantry. An old adding machine and blank checks transported us to a world far away from the den where we often played. I loved the way she would let me have the last sip of her coffee—mostly coffee-soaked sugar granules by the time I had a taste—and I wonder if it's part of why I still covet my daily cup to this day. There were no electronics or distractions to divert attention from truly "being" in those moments.

Summers seemed made for running around the yard. Adventures were created, and stories were spun across the little "bridge to nowhere" tucked under the large, shady tree. Gleeful laughter accompanied wistful swinging on the creaky front porch rocker. A butterfly she named Pretty used to stop by to visit. Convinced it was her each time, she'd speak tenderly, saying, "Why, hello, Pretty! How are you today?"

She told me once that Pretty could tell us of her adventures "beyond the porch." We loved spinning stories, sharing about where she had been. Pretty would always come back—each time changed—having experienced new people, places, and things. We'd interpret her travels, breathing stories to life with awe and wonder. We'd laugh, rocking there on the porch, my head often resting in the comforting nook of her arm.

Perhaps that's how it is with us too—the gift of being nurtured and cared for. Given the space to shift and grow, we fly away and return again. Often, we are changed. It can be easy to take this gift for granted or forget this endless cycle of change requires care and nurturing. Author, speaker, and leadership expert John C. Maxwell reminds us, "Nurturing has the ability to transform people's lives" (Maxwell 2010, 274).

Nurture: the final core value in a recipe to ALIGN with change as a lifestyle. Defined by *Oxford Languages* (2023) as *"the process of caring for and encouraging the growth or development of someone or something,"* it may not be difficult to understand why it's an essential core value to living in change. The "care" part of nurturing asks us to consider what's needed as we grow and shift. Its "encouragement" allows us to determine what is important to eliminate from our environment so we continue to thrive.

In their research on the role of nurturing environments in promoting human well-being, Anthony Biglan et al. share their findings on the importance and value of creating and supporting nurturing environments. They identify the four factors of these environments that promote and support human well-being:

First, these environments minimize biologically and psychologically toxic events. Second, they teach, promote, and richly reinforce prosocial behavior, including self-regulatory behaviors and all the skills needed to become productive adult members of society. Third, they monitor and limit opportunities for problem behavior. Fourth, they foster psychological flexibility—the ability to be mindful of one's thoughts and feelings and act in the service of one's values, even when one's thoughts and feelings discourage taking valued action (Biglan et al. 2012).

Their findings call for a paradigm shift in how we value the health and well-being of our future society. Currently, the primary focus is on attending to the needs of individual problems. Ultimately, this approach applies Band-Aids to issues rather than discovering and addressing the root causes of a problem. The shifts needed to drastically reduce the systemic challenges of academic failure, crime, mental illness, abuse and neglect, drug addiction, risky sexual behavior, poverty, and even physical illness require nurturing environments to become a cultural habit. Establishing and maintaining this ideal means attending to who we are while investing in who we want to be.

Nurturing, like growth or change, isn't just about setting up and completing a list of ideal circumstances. Once we check off the boxes and finish our to-do lists, we might be tempted to go on with our day. Nurturing is a long-term commitment to caring for and attending to that requires us to be present and aware.

We can look to nature for inspiration and guidance. Like so many creatures in the natural world, we are constantly in adaptive cycles. These cycles, whether lasting a day, a month, or a period of years, ask us to pay attention to their rhythms. We nurture ourselves when we commit to this act of attending to these cycles. Sometimes it can feel like we are riding waves. There are natural ebbs and flows, highs and lows, and there are inevitable periods of breakdown as we prepare to create or become something new.

A snake sheds its skin when it has outgrown it, when it is no longer helpful, or, in some cases, to proactively avoid parasites. When this process occurs, the snake's new skin must form before the old one is shed. Although it's a necessary part of the cycle, a period in the transition leaves the snake temporarily unable to see well, or even blind. Sometimes the snake must find a safe place to hide until they are ready to shed the old skin. Once shed, the skin that is no longer needed is discarded until the process repeats itself. At that point, the snake will once again shed, each time forming a new skin that adapts to its ongoing needs, whether changes in size, shape, or circumstance.

For hermit crabs, shells aren't just a decorative accessory but a necessary protection. Hermit crabs' process of molting, where they leave and find a new shell, supports their growth and evolution, but it also leaves them incredibly vulnerable. Having no protection without their shell, they will often bury themselves in the sand during this transition period to ensure their safety. They undergo this process in regular cycles every twelve to eighteen months.

And then, of course, there's the butterfly. Butterflies are one of nature's most shining examples of transformation. The process of a caterpillar turning into a butterfly is a metamorphosis. Growing up with Eric Carle's story of *The Very Hungry Caterpillar*, it was a thrill to read along as the caterpillar worked his way through the greatest feast imaginable. Then, feeling plenty full, he spun a cocoon. After some time, he emerged as a beautiful butterfly. But the true process of metamorphosis is delicate and intricate—a far cry from this hungry caterpillar's glamorized version.

For the full transformation from caterpillar to butterfly to occur, the caterpillar must completely break down. In fact, if you were to break open the cocoon at a certain point in the cycle, there would be nothing left but a gooey mess of cells. Present in the caterpillar's DNA from inception, its cells retain a vision of what it will become. These imaginal discs survive the breakdown and help fuel the next phase of growth and change. The system discards what is no longer necessary and begins generating what is needed to move the process forward. It's clear this creature was designed to live out the embodiment of metamorphosis—to break down, change, grow, and ultimately emerge as a butterfly.

Transformational life and leadership coach Kelly Wendorf applies this phenomenon of metamorphosis to the ongoing journey of change and transformation in her work at Thunderbird Ridge, the home of her business EQUUS in Santa Fe, New Mexico. Her book, *Flying Lead Change: 56 Million Years of Wisdom for Leading and Living*, offers an approach to leading and living inspired by two profound sources of ancient wisdom: indigenous peoples and *equus* (Latin for horse). Sitting down and speaking with Wendorf, she shared her understanding of growth and evolution: "We are wired to transform—to be a part of the 3.8 billion years of evolutionary intelligence that is nature. We're a part of nature. And nature is always evolving and changing and growing." Her words are a reminder we can learn from the examples of adaptive transformation and evolution cycles as they reveal themselves and apply them to our experience.

Fortunately, we don't have to break down to a cellular level of caterpillar goo to transform into our own version of a butterfly. But we do often experience a breaking down of sorts. In that process, there is an inevitable letting go required. Much like the caterpillar reforming as a butterfly, we determine what can be discarded and what will be needed for us to move forward. The concept of imaginal cells helps remind us we can trust in the vision of who we are to become.

This period of breaking down and letting go during our process of transformation is what Wendorf refers to as the "messy middle." It's a time when we have solidly broken down who we were but aren't yet entirely sure who we will be. The vulnerability of this phase of becoming, like the caterpillar reimagining and regenerating into a butterfly, requires deep nurturing. This is kind nurturing that also invites growth through care and encouragement through compassion.

Once more, we return to the exploration of how we can deepen our ability to live in and ALIGN with change. We have the choice and privilege to consider how this core value can be honored and strengthened in our lives. As we have seen through Authenticity, Learning, Intentionality, Gratitude, and now Nurturing, in each quality an invitation remains present to discover what can be offered to us on our journey.

Nurturing honors:	And is:
Self	Kind
Process	Caring
Feelings	Compassionate

Deep nurturing may mean taking care of our physical self by giving our body the food, sleep, and sustenance it needs. We might attend to our emotional selves by spending time with people who see, support, understand, and embrace us for who, and where, we are in our process. We can nurture our mental selves by deciding what narratives we want to entertain and attending to the thought patterns and habits we choose. We are always careful to notice where judgment, self-criticism, and sabotage may sneak in.

Nurturing choices in action can sometimes look like:

- Recognizing the need to let go of long-time friendships or circles of friends as our own priorities and needs shift.
- Leaving a stable job to start your own business, even at the risk of failure.
- Setting clear boundaries in a familial or intimate relationship that is unhealthy or unfulfilling.
- Eliminating "dishonest kindnesses" such as saying "yes" to that lunch or committing to a project where there isn't time, energy, or interest.

Nurturing asks us to look inward and, with compassion, offer ourselves time and space to truly attend to our own needs. It isn't always easy, but it's a necessary part of becoming. Much different than simply offering ourselves an escape from our current circumstances, this becoming is self-actualization; a true metamorphosis that allows us to emerge into the next version of who we are.

In the 2006 documentary *Kanyini* (Hogan 2006), Uncle Bob Randall, a custodial elder of the Uluru in Australia, shares his story, history, and culture. Kanyini, a principle of connectedness through caring and responsibility that underpins Aboriginal life, describes both a way of life and a way of being. It offers guiding principles for living in harmony with the earth and each other in community. Interconnection between one's belief system, spirituality, the land, and family doesn't just offer purpose but represents life.

Colonization meant many of the customs and ways of the Aboriginal peoples were stifled. Freedoms were stolen when they were harshly displaced from their lands. Still, the strength and power of forty thousand years of culture models a concept that unites all things. Kanyini is connection and meaning, and understanding and living the Kanyini principles can support deeper connections in our modern world. It is a principle that embraces balance and harmony through its deep sense of commitment. Living it results in a nurturing way of life for both people and land and attends to the nature of our beingness in the world.

Uncle Bob Randall was a friend and mentor to Kelly Wendorf, integral in inviting many wise teachings which informed and enriched her life and work. In her book, *Flying Lead Change*, she describes Kanyini as "the notion of unconditional love, born of the recognition of our connection with all things, and therefore our responsibility to all things" (Wendorf 2020, 49). In conversation, I ask how she believes the concepts of Kanyini and nurturing intertwine. She answered: "If we are going to care for others and take accountability and responsibility for the greater whole, then we are a part of that greater whole. We must care for ourselves too. There's a strong fidelity when we're responsible to ourselves because nobody else is going to be. It's really understanding that this vehicle in life—this vehicle as in this body—and this life are so precious. My nurturing needs to be in service to that fidelity. Of my becoming."

Becoming is a process that often takes us to places we may not have known to dream of, and our journey may not always appear as we may have planned. Sitting cross-legged in the front of the room, Ashley gracefully bows as she shares a reverent "namaste" with her students. She walked into her first yoga class over twenty years earlier. Even after decades of practicing and teaching yoga, she still considers herself, first and foremost, a student and a curious learner. Now more than just her happy place, her mat greets her daily with questions, challenges, and opportunities for deep connection. Her practice, like her, tells a story of evolving, shifting, and transformation.

Arriving where she is today hasn't been a journey that followed a linear path. In fact, in many moments her process of transformation seemed anything but kind and compassionate. Eight years prior, she was hit by a car while crossing the street. Breaking her pelvis in three places, the accident forced her to stop entirely. Listening to her body was no longer a luxury but an essential part of her daily existence. She was in a wheelchair, unable to walk. The left side of her body was broken and required skillful care and intense rehabilitation. Ashley had to learn how to nurture herself deeply.

As she worked on healing, personal setbacks in relationships and jobs, health complications, and the loss of loved ones plagued the following years. Strengthening and growth seemed painfully slow. It seemed when one thing built up, another area of her life would fall into ruin. Still, in the wake of so many challenging life experiences, she found space for light and hope. Reminded of the potential that can exist, even in the wake of complete chaos and destruction, she recalls a quote from the movie *Eat, Pray, Love* that often returns to her: "Ruin is a gift. Ruin is the road to transformation" (Murphy 2010, 51:32).

A year and a half after the trauma left her unable to walk, she was proud of her healing. She had regained the use of her body and was once again able to walk. A left side that was once broken could now hold her firmly as she carefully flowed through sun salutations on her mat. She traveled to Bali, feeling pulled to immerse herself in her passion for yoga. She deepened her sense of connection to something bigger than herself. It was a crucial point in her growth—physically, mentally, and spiritually. Forced to relinquish control of her life as it had been, she trusted deeply in the inner knowing that something greater was ahead.

Ashley came back changed. Her body renewed and strengthened with the support of family, friends, doctors, and specialists. Committing to her ongoing growth, she relentlessly attended to her physical, mental, and spiritual health. She chose to nurture her needs daily. "Over the years, I've learned to set firm and healthy boundaries. I've learned that saying 'no' is a complete sentence. I've also learned having the right humans in my inner circle to support and encourage the balance I strive to maintain makes saying 'yes' easy."

Ashley's story is one of evolution and becoming. Deep nurturing came with change she didn't ask for but showed up in her life as a humble teacher. With each transformation and subsequent emergence, she gave space to honor what needed to be shed: one breath, one pose, and one shape at a time. She shared with me a sentiment she often shares with her students, a reminder of choice on our journey toward growth and change: "We have the opportunity to embrace every challenge with gratitude and grace. Just as there is light in the dark, there is beauty in chaos. We are evolution in constant motion."

On a sunny Sunday afternoon in late February 2020, the warm California sun greeted my face while crowds of people milled around. My friend and I browsed the Hollywood Walk, taking in endless rows of names, stars, and handprints. Memorialized for a time in cement, those imprints seemed permanent, although, over the years, I'm sure they have been replaced as many times as was necessary. I leaned down to pose for a picture, an excited tourist smiling big and bold. A gentle tickle and light flutter grazed my forehead as I stood up. Right at my third eye, a butterfly had landed.

My friend exclaimed, "Oh my gosh. Hold still!" She frantically snapped a few photos, capturing the rare moment we were sure wouldn't last.

The butterfly just rested there. Not wanting to scare or disturb my newly settled friend, I stood in what felt like an endless state of perfect pause. I knew I would never have this moment, or this exact version of myself, again. *Savor. Be with this.*

Eventually, the butterfly fluttered away, but in that moment of connection I could offer her a safe place to land. Returning home, she could rest and nurture before she went off on another adventure. Maybe it was my grandmother sending me a reminder of Pretty and our shared memories. Butterflies signify spiritual growth and transformation. Whatever our moment was, it gave her and I exactly what we needed.

There was no way to know it then, but that was the last trip I would take for some time. Not even two weeks later, the world went into a state of lockdown due to the COVID-19 crisis, which resulted in a pandemic. This set of circumstances indirectly began my most recent journey of observing these spaces and cycles of change. I watched as the world displayed a staggering amount of adaptability, resilience, and courage in the wake of such an unexpected and life-altering time. Even through fear and the unknown, change began to emerge. On a personal level, it catalyzed a series of evolutions and transformations in my own life: a move halfway across the country, a deeper exploration of my own healing and growth journey, and writing this book.

None of this would have happened without choosing to lean into my life, even when I wasn't sure what was ahead. In her book *Lean Forward Into Your Life: Listen Hard, Live With Intention, and Play With Abandon*, Mary Anne Radmacher titles one of her chapters, "Walk to the Edge." It begins with words that have stuck with me for many years since I came across them. "It is not the easy or convenient life for which I search, but life lived to the edge of all that I may be. One always meets their destiny on the way to somewhere else. At first glance, it may appear too hard. Look again. Always look again" (2015, n.p).

This dance of life—this journey—is laden with change. Unknowns, stretches, barriers and breakthroughs lead us to crossroads that require permission and ask us to shift our perspective. We move, adapt, align, and change. Ultimately, we become. We become the next version of ourselves that will take us further along the road of life.

I don't know where my next steps will take me. I never can. But I move forward confidently, knowing I have the tools, skills, and core values to support a life truly aligned with change. Moving toward the unknown is part of my yet-unwritten story, and the pathways ahead are mine to design, build, and embrace.

CONCLUSION

Getting "There"

For three years, I had faithfully descended the stairs at 508 East Washington Street. The rituals of the morning routine offered comfort and respite. Shoes and coats were left lined up just inside the upstairs entry door. The first person to arrive turned on the hot pot, whose invitational bubbling reminded me something was always simmering just up ahead. I sat cradling a steaming mug of tea as sunlight streamed in through the basement windows, casting a warm glow on the cedar-covered walls. Each day was guided by the familiar wisdom of my teachers, Joan and Alex. Their life's work and teaching were deeply embedded in the tenants of curiosity, learning, and exploration. They were approaching their eighties when I was training to become a teacher of the Alexander Technique. Yet the way they embodied the work's principles made their experience seem youthful: limitless and full of possibility.

Daily physical explorations supported a room full of eager students as we deepened our sense of embodied understanding. The principles of the Alexander Technique offered the tools to explore and apply the process of change to the physical body, which translated to so many other areas of life. I gained tremendous skills as I discovered these keys to explore and facilitate change. Thinking in action not only became a choice but a new habit, one that would open my life to continual opportunities for conscious growth. A naive part of me was convinced after three years and 1600 hours of hands-on training, I'd "have it." Arriving at the end of the yellow brick road, I'd reach the glimmering Land of Oz, knowing precisely what it meant to change. Instead, crossing the threshold from student to teacher only seemed to bring questions:

- *Where do I begin?*
- *Do I know enough to change? Will I ever know enough?*
- *Where do I go from here?*

Finding answers to these questions led me to an exploration of change I never expected. I found the Alexander Technique because of a choice I knew I had to make at eighteen years old. I didn't know what I was going to learn. Remaining curious, I considered what I didn't (yet) know. I started out to solve a different problem and stumbled on the indirect pathway of what it means to live in change. It's an ongoing adventure that seems to choose me just as much as I make choices each step along the way.

A kind of paralysis can result from being unsure of how to process the seemingly unending number of options in front of us. We can get caught in a loop of confusion and overwhelm if we feel we "don't know." But acknowledging we don't know is sometimes the best place to start, especially if that's where we are. If we start with where we are, we've already made an important choice. Things begin to open up.

With each choice, there is a renewed freedom to start again. In this simple act, the process is not just a reaction but an interaction, an exploration, or even a dance. Pathways begin to emerge. Some arise from connections we have already established and explored. Others seem newly illuminated. The inevitable give and take—back and forth—of the journey is something we can not only embrace but also enjoy. This continuous pursuit of uncovering the change process drove me to ask new questions, which I explored through the three parts of this book:

- *Why change?*
- *What does it mean to change now?*
- *How do I keep changing, growing, evolving, and becoming?*

Many people think they don't have the tools or skills to change and change is simply about what happens to them. Instead, I choose to believe knowledge is power. When we are aware of the things holding us back, we can establish the optimal conditions for change. When we determine what tools can support us in our process, we have a clearer sense of where to begin.

Stretch, Permission, and Perspective are interwoven with The Change Cycle to support this ongoing unfolding. This brings us closer to the growth we want in our lives. To make change sustainable, we establish core values that support our ability to *ALIGN* with change. The aim is progress, not perfection. It's about the journey, not the destination. One of the most simple yet profound ways this happens is through choice.

My teachers, Joan and Alex, modeled a way of living, teaching, and supporting change. They offered me a gift I wouldn't wholly understand for many years. The pervasive comfort of their constant presence and steady hands modeled what it meant to "be with" someone exactly as they are, without judgment. Their commitment to ongoing discovery created continuous opportunities for me to grow and change. Slowly, I learned what it meant to step into the power of intentional thinking and conscious choice. I'm reminded of the simple words of the Giver in Lois Lowry's novel of the same name. While his young pupil, Jonas, grapples with what it means to learn, understand, and embrace his path, the Giver aims to offer counsel—suggesting the freedom to choose is perhaps more important than the result of any choice. He gently offers, "It's the choosing that's important, isn't it?" (Lowry 2011, 99).

It *is* the choosing that's important. The freedom to choose is a gift, with each choice leading us to where we are at this exact moment. Embracing the unknown isn't about having all the answers. It's about recognizing that sometimes more questions are the key to the next step on our journey. Pause for a moment and see what pathways appear. Take a deep breath and start moving. Once you've chosen to embrace change, the rest of the story remains yours to write.

Acknowledgments

As a child, I was a voracious reader. Pages of words enlivened worlds in my mind. I had little desire to do anything else in my free time and would scour the library for new books each week. Even into adulthood, I would happily stay up all night, sacrificing precious sleep (yes, I am a solid "need-eight-hours-a-night" type) to finish reading. These storied journeys' gripping, frustrating, or emotional conclusions became much more than entertainment. They were versions of life I could dive into, get lost in, and feel from the inside out.

Words have remained a favorite medium through the years. Friends and family are familiar with the cards I often send. Whether in celebration, sympathy, or just because, I have always chosen my words carefully. In dark moments, my soul finds solace in pouring words onto pages that (somehow) emerge as meaningful expressions of truth. My desk is layered with handwritten scribbles filling notepads, journals, and Post-it notes. Each page holds precious ideas and endless inspiration. In a world where digital footprints can be washed away like sand on a beach, I dream that part of my legacy will be these messages left to be rediscovered by those who will come after me. I hope my words will empower and inspire others in their mission to change themselves—and the world.

There is absolutely no way (in hell!) this book could have made it out of my heart and into the world without an incredible amount of support. I'm beyond thankful for everyone listed below. Although I don't think words will ever be enough, I'll attempt to offer my gratitude and appreciation.

To all those in my life who have shown up for me in ways big and small through this process (you know who you are): The depth of your belief in me before this book was even fully formed is humbling. Thank you for sitting with me in the moments when I wasn't sure I could see my path forward. Thank you for holding big, safe spaces for my fears (and tears) and wildly celebrating successes. I appreciate your willingness to take on so many roles. Your contributions as thought partners, title brainstormers, idea generators, wordsmiths, and cheerleaders have been sustaining, and I hope each of you knows how much you mean to me. Most of all, thank you for understanding exactly when to lean in a little further and knowing when I needed my hand squeezed just a little bit tighter. I am forever grateful for your wisdom, which inspires me daily. You are such a big part of who I am today.

With special acknowledgment and my eternal gratitude to those willing to invest in me and this book journey, helping me reach my goals and become a published author: To my parents, Hank and Juliann DeAngelis; Baum Realty Group's David Baum and Mike Demetriou; and Will Liverman and Claudine Tambuatco: thank you for your incredibly generous support of this creative endeavor.

Additional special thanks to all the book's early supporters—every one of you has helped make this dream a reality:

Abby Rethwisch	Dasha Shor*
The Aeschliman-Palacios Family	David Allen
	Debbie Paterson
Alexander Konetzki	Debra Asis
Alexandra Kassouf*	Dianne Seaman
Allyna Steinberg	Donna Geschrey*
Amanda MacDonald	Dru Heidle
Amanda McDonnell	Elif Allenfort
Angela Geschrey	Elissa M. Baskovich
Anna Laurenzo	Enriqueta Perez-Somarriba
Anna Sobotka*	Eric Hartlauf
Anne Hungate*	Eric Koester
Ashley Comforte	Eric Shulz
Ashley George	Erik Bendix
Barbara Kinnas	Erika Knierim
Brian Shumaker*	Francis Kasi
Brittany Loewen	Glenna Batson
Candice DelPrete	Greg and Abby Davis
Carmella Comforte	Hannah Austin
Carolyn Boudreau	Heather Towt
Carrie Abner	Hugo Valverde
Carol S. Wray	Ilana Weinstein
Cassandra Smalley	Isabel Leonard
Cherie Balsamo	Jacob Angel*
Chris and Iku DeAngelis*	Jacqueline Magill
Chris Hanig	Jameson James
Christi Daniels	Jean Spellman
Constance Bonbrest	Dr. Jennie Byrne
Dana Hotle	Jennifer Kosharsky

Jerry Beno
Joe Michalak
John Kelly
John Thompson III
Jonathan and Heidi Leathwood
Joyce Griggs*
Julie Brigham
Justin Bandy
The Kammer Family
Karen Shulz*
Katherine Getz
Kathleen Beardsley*
Kelly Kruse
Kelly Sundberg
Kevin DeAngelis
Kim Warriner*
Kimberly Robertson
Kristen Bigham
Kristen Tocci
Laura Cvitkovich and Mitch Hodge*
Laura Guili
Lauren Bartleson
Lauretta Webb*
Laurie Geschrey
Lawrence Brownlee
Lena Dickinson
Lindsay Martin
Maria Webb
Marlon "International" Mills

Martha Hadjidakis
Matt Hensrud
Matthew Fetter*
Megan Dunlay
Megan Gilette
Meighan Leibert
Melissa Renner
Meridith Grundei
Michael Kelly
Michael Walters
Mike Demetriou
The Mohr Family
Molly Hensrud*
Molly Kamykowski
Monika Gross
Nadya Ichinomiya
Nancy Maguire
Nancy Sosnowski
Natalie Pace Amrany*
Natalie Wood
Neil V. Shah
Nicki Sutcliffe
Nicole Olmo*
The Poulos Family
Reese Land
Rick Carbaugh*
Rob Laragh
Ryan Carpenter
Sandi Silvious
Sarah Rogers Morris
Sarah Toennis
Scott Profeta

Shalini Trehan
Shannon Shin*
Sheena Wolinski
Stasia Forsythe Siena
Dr. Stephanie Dixon
Susan Claus
Suzanne Kensington*

Theodore Tabe
Thomas Nolan
Tina and Steve Fischer*
William Delanoy
Yasemin Ipek Blanton
Yvonne Redman

Denotes individuals who purchased multiple copies

To the support teams at The Creator Institute and New Degree Press: Thank you for your commitment to furthering new voices and supporting first-time authors through an incredible journey. Special appreciation to Eric Koester and Shanna Heath for their encouragement, motivation, and expertise, to my invaluable (and patient!) editors Catherine Sigler and Ken Cain, as well as Sherman Morrison, Brian Bies, and all the talented and creative individuals in copy editing, proofreading, layout, design, and marketing who helped birth this book into the world.

To the teachers and mentors who have supported my personal journey of healing, growth, and transformation: Words cannot express my gratitude. To Stasia Forsythe Siena, my first teacher, who introduced me to the Alexander Technique and its invaluable principles of change in action, and our teachers Joan and Alex Murray for their lifelong commitment to growth and learning; to Dr. Valerie Rein and Jeffrey Tambor, Kelly Wendorf and the herd at Equus, the women of the Artemis Wisdom Circle and The Thriving Circle; and to Niall Kelly, Shelley Maddox, Kevin and Jessica Oberhausen, and Robin Woodward. Thank you for showing me that healing, growth, and change (although not for the faint of heart) can always be explored with meaningful intention and kindness toward oneself.

To the amazing individuals who contributed to the contents of this book, trusting me to share their stories and words on these pages: I'm not sure my words would have the same effects without the resonance of your experience. I know you will inspire so many others, just as you have deeply inspired me. Thank you for trusting me to translate your magic and brilliance onto these pages.

And to all the future readers of this book—those brave enough to venture out into unknown territory: May exploring and embracing your yet uncharted pathways lead to your boldest becomings.

About the Author

As an innovative and strategic thinker, Lisa DeAngelis has applied a broad array of experiences to inform her intuitive approach to "doing" life. Walking with individuals through the meaningful intersections of their lives is an integral part of her purpose and mission. She's always valued expressing herself through words, and becoming a published author is the culmination of a dream she once thought unattainable.

Lisa has lived in New York City since April 2021 after spending the previous decade living in Chicago. As a certified teacher of the Alexander Technique since 2009, she has worked with an extensive clientele of musicians, actors, athletes, and medical and business professionals. She has coached women through personal and career transitions, supporting them in embracing change and living their best lives.

Lisa works professionally in private personal management and is committed to leading authentically and living with intention. She is proud of her daily mindfulness practices, meaningful relationships, and capacity to support the things, people, and causes she is passionate about (including opera and the arts). She loves preparing (and enjoying!) good food, has a weakness for a well-made drink, and is always up for a cup of coffee.

For more about Lisa, please visit: www.LisaDeAngelis.com

Appendix

INTRODUCTION

DeGusta, Michael. 2012. "Are Smart Phones Spreading Faster than Any Technology in Human History?" *MIT Technology Review* (March). https://www.technologyreview.com/2012/05/09/186160/are-smart-phones-spreading-faster-than-any-technology-in-human-history/.

CHAPTER 1

Atkinson, Brooks. 1951. *Once Around the Sun*. United States: Harcourt, Brace.

Carroll, Lewis. 1920. *Alice's Adventures in Wonderland*. United Kingdom: W.B. Conkey, 1920.

Eidelman, Scott, Jennifer Pattershall, and Christian S. Crandall. 2010. "Longer Is Better." *Journal of Experimental Social Psychology* 46, no. 6 (November): 993–98. https://doi.org/10.1016/j.jesp.2010.07.008.

Lewin, Kurt. 1947. "Frontiers in group dynamics: II. Channels of group life; social planning and action research." *Human relations* 1, no. 2 (November): 143–153. https://doi.org/10.1177/001872674700100201.

Pew Research Center. 2021. "Social Media Fact Sheet." *Pew Research Center: Internet, Science & Tech*. April 7, 2021. https://www.pewresearch.org/internet/fact-sheet/social-media/.

Robinson, T.M., ed. 1987. *Heraclitus: Fragments*. United Kingdom: University of Toronto Press.

U.S. Census Bureau. "Monthly Business Applications." Business Formation Statistics, May 13, 2019, graph 1. Accessed April 28, 2022. https://www.census.gov/econ/bfs/index.html.

Venus, Merlijn, Daan Stam, and Daan van Knippenberg. 2019. "Visions of Change as Visions of Continuity." *Academy of Management Journal* 62, no. 3 (June): 667–90. https://doi.org/10.5465/amj.2015.1196.

CHAPTER 2

Bode, Stefan, Anna Hanxi He, Chun Siong Soon, Robert Trampel, Robert Turner, and John-Dylan Haynes. 2011. "Tracking the Unconscious Generation of Free Decisions Using Ultra-High Field Fmri." *PLoS ONE* 6, no. 6 (June). https://doi.org/10.1371/journal.pone.0021612.

Clear, James. 2018. *Atomic Habits: An Easy & Proven Way to Build Good Habits & Break Bad Ones*. United States: Penguin Publishing Group.

Custers, Ruud, and Henk Aarts. 2010. "The Unconscious Will: How the Pursuit of Goals Operates Outside of Conscious Awareness." *Science* 329, no. 5987 (July): 47–50. https://doi.org/10.1126/science.1188595.

D'Angelo, Jonathan D., and Catalina L. Toma. 2016. "There Are Plenty of Fish in the Sea: The Effects of Choice Overload and Reversibility on Online Daters' Satisfaction with Selected Partners." *Media Psychology* 20, no. 1 (February): 1–27. https://doi.org/10.1080/15213269.2015.1121827.

Hanson, Rick. n.d. "Take in the Good." *Rick Hanson, Ph.D.* (blog). Accessed May 15, 2022. https://www.rickhanson.net/take-in-the-good/.

Koenig-Robert, Roger, and Joel Pearson. 2019. "Decoding the Contents and Strength of Imagery before Volitional Engagement." *Scientific Reports* 9, no. 1 (March). https://doi.org/10.1038/s41598-019-39813-y.

Kuhn, Gustav. 2019. "Mind Games: What Magic Reveals about How Our Brains Work." *The Guardian*. March 30, 2019. Accessed May 15, 2022. https://www.theguardian.com/lifeandstyle/2019/mar/30/mind-games-what-magic-reveals-about-how-our-brains-work.

Lally, Phillippa, Cornelia H. van Jaarsveld, Henry W. Potts, and Jane Wardle. 2009. "How Are Habits Formed: Modelling Habit Formation in the Real World." *European Journal of Social Psychology* 40, no. 6 (July): 998–1009. https://doi.org/10.1002/ejsp.674.

LePera, Nicole. 2021. *How to Do the Work: Recognize Your Patterns, Heal from Your Past, and Create Your Self*. United States: HarperCollins.

Martinez, Mario. 2014. *The MindBody Code: How to Change the Beliefs that Limit Your Health, Longevity, and Success*. United States: Sounds True. Kindle.

Nolfi, George, director. 2011. *The Adjustment Bureau*. Universal Pictures. 1 hr. 46 min. https://www.amazon.com/gp/video/detail/B00D5UKQCE.

"The Paradox of Choice." 2022. *The Decision Lab*. Accessed April 22, 2022. https://thedecisionlab.com/reference-guide/economics/the-paradox-of-choice.

Rein, Valerie. 2019. *Patriarchy Stress Disorder: The Invisible Inner Barrier to Women's Happiness and Fulfillment.* Ireland: Lioncrest Publishing.

Schwartz, Barry. 2009. *The Paradox of Choice: Why More Is Less, Revised Edition.* United States: HarperCollins. Hoopla.

Soon, Chun Siong, Anna Hanxi He, Stefan Bode, and John-Dylan Haynes. 2013. "Predicting free choices for abstract intentions." *Proceedings of the National Academy of Sciences,* 110, no. 15 (April): 6217–6222. https://doi.org/10.1073/pnas.1212218110

CHAPTER 3

Brown, Brené. 2013. *Daring Greatly: How the Courage to Be Vulnerable Transforms the Way We Live, Love, Parent, and Lead.* United Kingdom: Penguin Books Limited. Kindle.

Dictionary.com. s.v. "Resilience," accessed April 13, 2022. https://www.dictionary.com/browse/resilience.

Martin, Andrew J., Harry G. Nejad, Susan Colmar, and Gregory Arief Liem. 2013. "Adaptability: How Students' Responses to Uncertainty and Novelty Predict Their Academic and Non-Academic Outcomes." *Journal of Educational Psychology* 105, no. 3 (August): 728–46.
https://doi.org/10.1037/a0032794.

Merriam-Webster.com Dictionary, s.v. "courage," accessed January 5, 2023, https://www.merriam-webster.com/dictionary/courage.

Middleton, Eliza J., and Tanya Latty. 2016. "Resilience in Social Insect Infrastructure Systems." *Journal of The Royal Society Interface* 13, no. 116 (March). https://doi.org/10.1098/rsif.2015.1022.

Perel, Esther. n.d. "Letters From Esther #26: The Great Adaptation." *Esther Perel* (blog). Accessed February 19, 2022. https://www.estherperel.com/blog/letters-from-esther-26-the-great-adaptation.

Radmacher, Mary Anne. 2009. *Courage Doesn't Always Roar.* Ireland: Mango Media.

Rainie, Lee, and Janna Anderson. 2017. "Theme 2: Learners Must Cultivate 21stCentury Skills, Capabilities and Attributes." *Pew Research Center: Internet, Science & Tech.* May 3, 2017.
https://www.pewresearch.org/internet/2017/05/03/theme-2-learners-must-cultivate-21st.

Sarett, L. H. 1983. "Research and Invention." *Proceedings of the National Academy of Sciences of the United States of America* 80, no. 14 (July): 4572–74.
http://www.jstor.org/stable/14073.

CHAPTER 4

Barrett, Lisa Feldman. 2017. *How Emotions Are Made: The Secret Life of the Brain.* United States: Houghton Mifflin Harcourt.

Callaway, Naeem. n.d. *Goodreads*. Accessed December 15, 2022. https://www.goodreads.com/author/quotes/16655321.Naeem_Callaway.

Carleton, R. Nicholas. 2016. "Fear of the Unknown: One Fear to Rule Them All?" *Journal of Anxiety Disorders* 41 (June): 5–21. https://doi.org/10.1016/j.janxdis.2016.03.011.

Carleton, R. Nicholas. 2016. "Into the Unknown: A Review and Synthesis of Contemporary Models Involving Uncertainty." *Journal of Anxiety Disorders* 39 (April): 30–43. https://doi.org/10.1016/j.janxdis.2016.02.007.

Conley, Chip. 2012. *Emotional Equations: Simple Truths for Creating Happiness + Success*. United States: Atria Books.

D'Elia, Bill and Tony Pelan, directors. 2014. Season 10 Episode 24, "Fear (of the Unknown)." ABC. TV. 43 min.

"The Donkey in the Well." n.d. Accessed January 7, 2023. http://www.whitehorsestudio.com/dusty/fable_well.html.

Eliot, Thomas Stearns. 1931. In *Transit of Venus*, by Harry Crosby, Paris: Black Sun.

Grupe, Dan W, and Jack B Nitschke. 2013. "Uncertainty and anticipation in anxiety: an integrated neurobiological and psychological perspective." *Nature reviews. Neuroscience* vol. 14, 7 (June): 488–501. doi:10.1038/nrn3524.

Hendricks, Gay. 2009. *The Big Leap: Conquer Your Hidden Fear and Take Life to the Next Level*. United Kingdom: HarperCollins.

Lovecraft, H. P. 2013. *Supernatural Horror in Literature*. United Kingdom: Wermod and Wermod Publishing Group.

Santat, Dan. 2017. *After the Fall (How Humpty Dumpty Got Back Up Again)*. United States: Roaring Brook Press.

Schawbel, Dan. 2012. "How Emotional Equations Can Change Your Life." *Forbes*. January 13, 2012. https://www.forbes.com/sites/danschawbel/2012/01/12/how-emotional-equations-can-change-your-life/.

Topel, Fred. 2019. "'Frozen 2': What Awaits Olaf in the Enchanted Forest?" *Showbiz Cheat Sheet*. November 5, 2019. https://www.cheatsheet.com/entertainment/frozen-2-what-awaits-olaf-in-the-enchanted-forest.html/.

CHAPTER 5

Bennett, Roy T. 2020. *The Light in the Heart: Inspirational Thoughts for Living Your Best Life*. United States. Kindle.

Farber, Barry J. 2003. *Diamond Power: Gems of Wisdom from America's Greatest Marketer*. United States: Career Press.

Peers, Alexandra. 2018. "This New York Landmark's History Is More Compelling than Fiction." *Architectural Digest.* May 23, 2018.
https://www.architecturaldigest.com/story/met-opera-lincoln-center-history.

Webb, Thomas L., and Paschal Sheeran. 2006. "Does Changing Behavioral Intentions Engender Behavior Change? A Meta-Analysis of the Experimental Evidence." *Psychological Bulletin* 132, no. 2 (March): 249–68.
https://doi.org/10.1037/0033-2909.132.2.249.

CHAPTER 6

Howes, Lewis. 2016. "Greatness is living life outside of your comfort zone." Facebook. Accessed April 10, 2016.

https://www.facebook.com/lewishowes/photos/a.141646989224496/977780048944515/.

Howes, Lewis. 2012. *The Ultimate Webinar Marketing Guide.* Lewis Howes. Kindle.

Storr, Farrah. 2018. "The Discomfort Zone." Filmed April 2018 in Exeter, United Kingdom. TED video. 14:09.
https://www.youtube.com/watch?v=o4kcpVjw89c.

Taylor, Felicia. 2012. "Google's Marissa Mayer: Passion Is a Gender-Neutralizing Force." *CNN.* April 5, 2012. Accessed November 28, 2022.
https://www.cnn.com/2012/04/05/tech/google-marissa-mayer/index.html.

Woolley, Kaitlin, and Ayelet Fishbach. 2022. "Motivating Personal Growth by Seeking Discomfort." *Psychological Science* 33, no. 4 (March): 510–23.
https://doi.org/10.1177/09567976211044685.

Yerkes, Robert M., and John D. Dodson. 1908. "The Relation of Strength of Stimulus to Rapidity of Habit-Formation." *Journal of Comparative Neurology and Psychology* 18, no. 5 (November): 459–82.
https://doi.org/10.1002/cne.920180503.

CHAPTER 7

Brown, Brené. 2017. *Braving the Wilderness: The Quest for True Belonging and the Courage to Stand Alone.* United States: Random House Publishing Group.

Clear, James. 2022. "3-2-1: New Paths, the Danger of Complexity, and Making Fast Decisions." *James Clear* (blog). February 17, 2022.
https://jamesclear.com/3-2-1/february-17-2022.

Edmondson, Amy C., and Zhike Lei. 2014. "Psychological Safety: The History, Renaissance, and Future of an Interpersonal Construct." *Annual Review of Organizational Psychology and Organizational Behavior* 1, no. 1 (January): 23–43.
https://doi.org/10.1146/annurev-orgpsych-031413-091305.

Gilbert, Elizabeth. 2010. *Eat Pray Love: One Woman's Search for Everything Across Italy, India and Indonesia.* United States: Penguin Publishing Group.

Gilliard, Corinne, Heather McGinley, Laura Berger, Rachel Pikelny, and Lindsay Flader, producers. 2014. Season 5 Episode 27, "Elizabeth Gilbert: Give Yourself Permission to Honor Your Life." OWN. TV.

Porges, Stephen. W. 2017. *The Pocket Guide to the Polyvagal Theory: The transformative power of feeling safe* (Norton Series on Interpersonal Neurobiology). United Kingdom: W. W. Norton. Kindle.

Porges, Stephen W. 2009. "The Polyvagal Theory: New Insights into Adaptive Reactions of the Autonomic Nervous System." *Cleveland Clinic Journal of Medicine* 76, no. 4 suppl 2 (February). https://doi.org/10.3949/ccjm.76.s2.17.

CHAPTER 8

Covey, Stephen R. 2013. *The 7 Habits of Highly Effective People: Powerful Lessons in Personal Change.* United Kingdom: Simon & Schuster.

Cruz, Sadie. 2012. "A Boy and His Camera: A Q&A with Photography Powerhouse Rick Smolan." *TED* (blog). November 30, 2012. https://blog.ted.com/a-boy-and-his-camera-a-qa-with-photography-powerhouse-rick-smolan/.

Dweck, Carol S. 2007. *Mindset: The New Psychology of Success.* United States: Ballantine Books.

Killingsworth, Colleen. 2019. "'You Could Hear a Pin Drop': 650 Million People around the World Watched Man's First Steps on the Moon." *FOX 29 News Philadelphia.* July 19, 2019. Accessed June 20, 2022. https://www.fox29.com/news/you-could-hear-a-pin-drop-650-million-people-around-the-world-watched-mans-first-steps-on-the-moon.

Merriam-Webster.com Dictionary, s.v. "perspective," accessed January 5, 2023, https://www.merriam-webster.com/dictionary/perspective.

Reid, Guy, director. 2012. *Overview.* Planetary Collective. Vimeo, 19 min. https://vimeo.com/55073825.

Saltzberg, Barney. 2010. *Beautiful Oops!.* United Kingdom: Workman Publishing Company.

White, F. 1987. *The overview effect: Space exploration and human evolution.* Boston: Houghton Mifflin.

CHAPTER 9

Bernard, Barbara A., and Luanne Dowling. 2014. *Birthdays of the Soul: Seeing Yourself Change in Times of Sea Change.* Barbara Bernard and Luanne Dowling.

Hayes, Adele M., Jean-Philippe Laurenceau, Greg Feldman, Jennifer L. Strauss, and LeeAnn Cardaciotto. 2007. "Change Is Not Always Linear: The Study of Nonlinear and Discontinuous Patterns of Change in Psychotherapy." *Clinical Psychology Review* 27, no. 6 (July): 715–23. https://doi.org/10.1016/j.cpr.2007.01.008.

Prigogine, Ilya, and Isabelle Stengers. 1984. *Order out of chaos: Man's new dialogue with nature*. NY: Bantam Books.

CHAPTER 10

Benton, Elizabeth. 2019. *Chasing Cupcakes: How One Broke, Fat Girl Transformed Her Life (and How You Can, Too)*. United States: Primal Potential Publishing.

Ge, Long, Behnam Sadeghirad, Geoff D Ball, Bruno R da Costa, Christine L Hitchcock, Anton Svendrovski, Ruhi Kiflen, et al. 2020. "Comparison of Dietary Macronutrient Patterns of 14 Popular Named Dietary Programmes for Weight and Cardiovascular Risk Factor Reduction in Adults: Systematic Review and Network Meta-Analysis of Randomised Trials." *BMJ*, 2020, m696. https://doi.org/10.1136/bmj.m696.

Grant, Adam (@AdamMGrant). 2022. "Big career decisions don't come with a map, but all you need is a compass. The right next move is the one that brings you a step closer to living your core values. In an unpredictable world, you can't make a master plan. You can only gauge whether you're on a meaningful path." Twitter, March 27, 2022, 11:52 a.m.

Research and Markets Ltd. 2021. "Global Weight Loss Products and Services Market 2021-2026." *Research and Markets - Market Research Reports*. July 2021. Accessed May 4, 2022. https://www.researchandmarkets.com/reports/5393446/global-weight-loss-products-and-services-market.

CHAPTER 11

Bailey, Erica R., Sandra C. Matz, Wu Youyou, and Sheena S. Iyengar. 2020. "Authentic Self-Expression on Social Media Is Associated with Greater Subjective Well-Being." *Nature Communications* 11, no. 1 (October). https://doi.org/10.1038/s41467-020-18539-w.

Brown, Brené. 2022. *The Gifts of Imperfection: 10th Anniversary Edition: Features a New Foreword and Brand-new Tools*. United States: Hazelden Publishing.

Casey, John. 2021. *MERIDIAN: A Raw Thoughts Book*. United States: PHiR Publishing.

Miller, Christine Mason. 2008. *Ordinary Sparkling Moments: Reflections on Success and Contentment*. United States: Christine Mason Miller.

Thomas, Sunil. 2020. "Council Post: How Digital Customer Data Is Boosting Beauty Industry Growth." *Forbes*. October 21, 2020. https://www.forbes.com/sites/forbesnycouncil/2019/07/18/how-digital-customer-data-is-boosting-beauty-industry-growth/.

Varga, Somogy, and Charles Guignon. 2020. "Authenticity." *The Stanford Encyclopedia of Philosophy*. Spring 2020 edition. United States: The Metaphysics Research Lab at Stanford University. https://plato.stanford.edu/entries/authenticity/.

Wang, Robert R. n.d. "Yinyang (Yin-Yang)." *Internet encyclopedia of philosophy*. United States: Loyola Marymount University. Accessed June 2, 2022. https://iep.utm.edu/yinyang/.

CHAPTER 12

Anderson, Kevin J., and Brian Herbert. 2003. *Dune: House Harkonnen.* United Kingdom: Random House Worlds.

Doidge, Norman. 2007. *The Brain That Changes Itself: Stories of Personal Triumph from the Frontiers of Brain Science.* United States: Penguin Publishing Group.

Doidge, Norman. 2015. *The Brain's Way of Healing: Remarkable Discoveries and Recoveries from the Frontiers of Neuroplasticity.* United States: Penguin Publishing Group.

Grisold, Thomas, Alexander Kaiser, and Julee Hafner. 2017. "Unlearning before Creating New Knowledge: A Cognitive Process." *ScholarSpace.* (January). https://scholarspace.manoa.hawaii.edu/items/f000035a-ead4-4f0e-9eee-086f48c740d8.

Holt, John Caldwell. 1978. *Never Too Late: My Musical Life Story.* New York: Delacorte Press.

Mackesy, Charlie. 2019. *The Boy, the Mole, the Fox and the Horse.* United States: HarperCollins.

O'Reilly, Barry. 2018. *Unlearn: Let Go of Past Success to Achieve Extraordinary Results.* United States: McGraw-Hill Education.

Scharmer, Otto C. 2009. *Theory U: Learning from the Future as It Emerges.* United Kingdom: Berrett-Koehler Publishers.

UMass Lowell. 2014. "Bill Nye, The Science Guy - UMass Lowell 2014 Commencement Morning Speaker." UMass Lowell. May 17, 2014. 32:27. https://www.youtube.com/watch?v=wzwX-qu5fRA.

Wu, Rachel, George W. Rebok, and Feng Vankee Lin. 2016. "A Novel Theoretical Life Course Framework for Triggering Cognitive Development across the Lifespan." *Human Development* 59, no. 6 (April): 342–65. https://doi.org/10.1159/000458720.

CHAPTER 13

Chang, Ruth. 2017. "Hard Choices." *Journal of the American Philosophical Association* 3, no. 1 (May): 1–21. https://doi.org/10.1017/apa.2017.7.

De Couck, Marijke, Ralf Caers, Liza Musch, Johanna Fliegauf, Antonio Giangreco, and Yori Gidron. 2019. "How Breathing Can Help You Make Better Decisions: Two Studies on the Effects of Breathing Patterns on Heart Rate Variability and Decision-Making in Business Cases." *International Journal of Psychophysiology* 139 (May): 1–9. https://doi.org/10.1016/j.ijpsycho.2019.02.011.

Funt, Juliet. 2021. *A Minute to Think: Reclaim Creativity, Conquer Busyness, and Do Your Best Work.* United States: HarperCollins.

Oxford Languages, s.v. "intentional," accessed January 5, 2023, https://www.google.com/search?q=intentional.

Samit, Jay. 2015. *Disrupt You! Master Personal Transformation, Seize Opportunity, and Thrive in the Era of Endless Innovation.* United States: Flatiron Books.

CHAPTER 14

Algoe, Sara B., Barbara L. Fredrickson, and Shelly L. Gable. 2013. "The Social Functions of the Emotion of Gratitude via Expression." *Emotion* 13, no. 4 (June): 605-9. https://doi.org/10.1037/a0032701.

Axelrod, Robert, and William D Hamilton. 1981. "The Evolution of Cooperation." *Science* 211, no. 4489 (March): 1390-96. https://www.jstor.org/stable/1685895.

Bunchman, Beth. 2016. *Cultivating Gratitude: A Guided Journal for a Positive Mindset.* Beth Bunchman.

de Waal, Frans B.M. 1997. "The Chimpanzee's Service Economy: Food for Grooming." *Evolution and Human Behavior* 18, no. 6 (November): 375-86. https://doi.org/10.1016/s1090-5138(97)00085-8.

den Heijer, Alexander. 2018. *Nothing You Don't Already Know: Remarkable Reminders about Meaning, Purpose, and Self-Realization.* United States: Alexander den Heijer.

Dossey, Larry. 2018. "The Helper's High." *EXPLORE* 14, no. 6 (November): 393-99. https://doi.org/10.1016/j.explore.2018.10.003.

Dunfield K. A. 2014. "A construct divided: Prosocial behavior as helping, sharing, and comforting subtypes." *Frontiers in Psychology* 5, 958. (September). http://dx.doi.org/10.3389/fpsyg.2014.00958.

Emmons, Robert. 2004. "The Psychology of Gratitude: An Introduction." In *The Psychology of Gratitude*, edited by Robert A. Emmons, and Michael E. McCullough, 3-16. United Kingdom: Oxford University Press.

Jans-Beken, Lilian, Nele Jacobs, Mayke Janssens, Sanne Peeters, Jennifer Reijnders, Lilian Lechner, and Johan Lataster. 2019. "Gratitude and Health: An Updated Review." *The Journal of Positive Psychology* 15, no. 6 (August): 743-82. https://doi.org/10.1080/17439760.2019.1651888.

Johnson, Lloyd Albert. 2004. *A Toolbox for Humanity: More Than 9000 Years of Thought.* United States: Trafford Publishing.

Trivers, Robert L. 1971. "The Evolution of Reciprocal Altruism." *The Quarterly Review of Biology* 46, no. 1 (March): 35-57. https://doi.org/10.1086/406755.

Voelkl, Bernhard, Steven J. Portugal, Markus Unsöld, James R. Usherwood, Alan M. Wilson, and Johannes Fritz. 2015. "Matching Times of Leading and Following

Suggest Cooperation through Direct Reciprocity during V-Formation Flight in Ibis." *Proceedings of the National Academy of Sciences* 112, no. 7 (February): 2115–20. https://doi.org/10.1073/pnas.1413589112.

Wong, Y. Joel, Jesse Owen, Nicole T. Gabana, Joshua W. Brown, Sydney McInnis, Paul Toth, and Lynn Gilman. 2016. "Does Gratitude Writing Improve the Mental Health of Psychotherapy Clients? Evidence from a Randomized Controlled Trial." *Psychotherapy Research* 28, no. 2 (May): 192–202. https://doi.org/10.1080/10503307.2016.1169332.

CHAPTER 15

Biglan, Anthony, Brian R. Flay, Dennis D. Embry, and Irwin N. Sandler. 2012. "The Critical Role of Nurturing Environments for Promoting Human Well-Being." *American Psychologist* 67, no. 4 (May-June): 257–71. https://doi.org/10.1037/a0026796.

Hogan, Melanie, director. 2006. "*Kanyini.*" Sand Hill Road Pictures. Vimeo, 52 minutes. https://vimeo.com/292549994.

Maxwell, John C. 2010. *Maxwell 2in1 (Developing the Leader W/in You/Developing Leaders Around You).* United States: Thomas Nelson.

Murphy, Ryan, director. 2010. *Eat Pray Love.* Columbia Pictures. Movie, 2 hr. 13 min. https://www.amazon.com/gp/video/detail/B00BR9YSBA.

Oxford Languages, s.v. "nurture," accessed January 5, 2023, https://www.google.com/search?q=nurture.

Radmacher, Mary Anne. 2015. *Lean Forward Into Your Life: Listen Hard, Live with Intention, and Play with Abandon.* Germany: Mango Media. Kindle.

Wendorf, Kelly. 2020. *Flying Lead Change: 56 Million Years of Wisdom for Leading and Living.* United States: Sounds True.

CONCLUSION

Lowry, Lois. 2011. *The Giver.* United States: Houghton Mifflin.

www.ingramcontent.com/pod-product-compliance
Lightning Source LLC
LaVergne TN
LVHW012014060526
838201LV00061B/4302